Roy Spilliers

March 2020

INDEX

PORTUGAL

INTRODUCTION

As we search for information on Portugal, it's easy to find heavy, tedious books disguised as travel guides that do not add any value to the tourist route. To meet with your expectations, our small local team has decided to go against the grain (as a proper Portuguese would do) and create a practical and functional guide full of experiences and specifically tailored information to lead you through the real Portugal.

Proud of the final work, we would like to express our most profound appreciation to those who voluntarily contributed to shaping this travel guide.

To be more aware of the tourists' immediate needs, we would be happy to hear your comments and suggestions, helping us to improve your experience. To provide feedback, you can contact us at the following email:
traveller@foxhoundglobal.com

We would also like to underline that by buying this guide, you are actively contributing to the SOS Children's Villages – Portugal; The world's largest non-governmental organization focused on supporting children without parental care and families at risk.

WHAT TO EXPECT

After analyzing most of the travel guides available in the market, we immediately decided what this publication should and should not be. In fact, as you dive into it, you'll find a ton of positive aspects, starting with the colloquial tone applied throughout.

Besides the practicality and functionality previously mentioned, you will find it very easy to read, as noncomplex historical details were used. To simplify your journey, the guide also comprises a variety of quick links that will redirect you to locations and to useful information regarding *Places to Visit*, the *Bucket List*, or even Hotels and Restaurants.

Our primary goal was to leave the exhaustive explanations behind and go into action, creating a connection with our readers. That's why you'll find a considerable number of thrilling adventures to embrace as you become a real *Tuga* (a proud Portuguese).

As you may understand, we have not experienced (yet) all the suggestions enclosed, but we can assure you that ALL of them, with no exception, came either from our experience or a local recommendation.

Although this has been a great investigative work, we most likely left something out. So, we challenge you to explore even more and discover what is missing. We are super excited to receive your individual feedback and vivid stories.

PORTUGAL IN A NUTSHELL

Located in Europe's southwest corner, surrounded by Spain and the Atlantic Ocean, Portugal has made its mark on the world. This small country was the first Nation to circumnavigate the Globe, bringing home unimaginable wealth, power, and influence. The Portuguese Empire lasted for six centuries and left behind tremendous traces of an abundant cultural heritage and artistic richness. Portugal's long history is now present in its imposing Castles and Walls that protected Kings, Queens, and fairytale

Palaces, bounded by enchanting and secluded forests and mountains.

This realm of grand plateaus and rugged landscapes also hosts 850 kilometers of sandy beaches bathed by the Atlantic and caressed by the warm Mediterranean winds.

Portugal is a country that needs to be deeply experienced to be understood, colored in vibrancy and youth, living intensely 24 hours a day. It is within this diversity, where the sophisticated cities contrast with ancient traditions, that rests some of the most friendly and hospitable people in Europe, never forgetting the audacity and excellence of its artists and athletes that have made Portugal world renowned.

This modern and progressive corner, blessed by Mother Nature and passionate by the eco-tourism, is also considered a privileged hot spot for birdwatching, surf, and golf. Here cooking has become a highly appreciated art and when conjugated with the world's best wines, can provide an outstanding feeling of relaxation and belonging.

Portugal has fostered a meaningful connection with the land, where people have the fortune to develop new passions and discover new ways of life. It is everything about getting off the beaten track and getting involved, experiencing new adventures, supported by the magnificence of the past and the excitement of the future.

Embark on a thrilling journey, take a deep breath, and dive into a marvelous and captivating country. Anchor to unforgettable memories and lose your heart to unique Portugal.

12 REASONS TO VISIT PORTUGAL

Although you may have already decided to come to Portugal having purchased this guide, we couldn't help but share our reasons to come. We feel deeply passionate about this beautiful country, and we're thrilled to share with you some of that love.

1 HISTORY
It is said that the Portuguese are descendants of nearly 20 different races that inhabited the Iberian Peninsula. You will discover its centenary and glorious past in every ancient castle, palace and religious landmark.

2 THE PEOPLE
The Portuguese are famous for their hospitality and kindness. Ask someone for directions, and minutes later you'll have dozens of passersby trying to help you enthusiastically.

3 BEAUTY
Portugal has 15 registered UNESCO World Heritage Sites, both rural and urban. Combine the green of nature with the deep blue of the sea, and you will find some of the most astonishing views in the world.

4 FOOD
Rich in meat and seafood dishes, your gastronomic universe will be widened by the variety and flavors of Portuguese cuisine. Don't even think about approaching a Portuguese restaurant on a strict diet!

5 WINE
Portugal is known for its fabulous Port wine, but that's just the tip of the iceberg. Here you will find a refined wine for every occasion and dozens of DOP wines – Controlled Designation of Origin.

6 WEATHER
Surrounded by the sea, Portugal was endowed with the best temperature in Europe. Imagine the inconvenience of having to carry along your sunglasses to protect you against the 250/300 days of sunshine per year.

7 TRADITIONS
Each city proudly organizes monumental festivities to remember the customs and traditions of the ancient times. The Portuguese are very proud of their roots and love to celebrate it through music and art.

8 BUDGET

Portugal is one of the least expensive countries in western Europe, allowing travelers to organize inexpensive trips from North to South. With a minimum wage of around 600€ per month, a high level of comfort can be easily maintained.

9 RELIGION

Built over rigorous religious beliefs, Portugal owns a wide range of Cathedrals, Convents, and Monasteries that totally integrate the landscape. The profound Catholic roots are responsible for most Portuguese traditions and festivals, making them magnanimous and worthy of experiencing.

10 MUSIC

Fado and regional folk music are some of the wealthiest art expressions of the country. Any self-respecting city in Portugal will offer live music performances every night.

11 SAFETY

Labelled one of the safest countries in the world, it's quite common for the locals to leave their houses, cars and wallets unlocked and unsupervised outside the major cities.

12 TECHNOLOGY

Portugal has countrywide high-speed internet coverage, superb governmental online services, and a world-leading electronic toll system. World technology behemoths, such as Google and Microsoft, are investing in the country, creating advanced infrastructures and mindset.

IMPORTANT HISTORICAL EVENTS

YEAR	EVENT
218 BC	Roman invasion
154 – 136 BC	*Viriato* resists the Roman invasion
711	The Iberian Peninsula is invaded by the Moorish
1095	*D. Henrique* receives the government of the *Condado Portucalense*
1128	*S. Mamede* battle
1143	Zamora treaty signed – Portugal independence. *D. Afonso Henriques* is named the first king
1249	Algarve's definitive conquest
1297	Alcanises treaty
1385	Aljubarrota battle. *Mestre de Avis* is claimed king of Portugal.
1415	Beginning of the Portuguese expansion. Conquest of Ceuta.
1572	Publication of *Os Lusíadas*, by *Luís de Camões*.
1578	Alcácel Quibir battle. *D. Sebastião* went missing
1581	*Filipe I* is the new king of Portugal
1640	Restauration of independence
1755	Lisboa's earthquake
1807	Beginning of the French invasion
1910	Republic implantation
1926	Beginning of the military dictatorship
1961	Beginning of the Ultramar war
1974	25th April – End of the military dictatorship
1986	Portugal enters CEE (European Union)
2002	Replacement of the *Escudo ($)* for the Euro (€)

ATLANTIC OCEAN

Bragança

Viana do Castelo

Braga

Vila Real

Porto

Aveiro   Viseu

Guarda

Coimbra

Castelo Branco

Leiria

Santarém   Portalegre

PORTUGAL

Lisboa

Évora

Setúbal

ESPAÑA

Beja

PORTUGAL ID

Faro

Capital:	Lisboa
Language:	Portuguese
Inhabitants:	10,3 million (2016)
Total Area:	92,212 km2
Currency:	€ (euro)
Religion:	90% Roman Catholic
Government structure:	Parliamentary system
Time zone:	GMT/UTC (+1 hour in Summer)
Drives on the:	Right
Driving License	_https://foxhoundglobal.com/yourls/driverslicenses_
Calling code:	+351

KNOW BEFORE YOU GO

CLIMATE AND PEAK TIME

Portugal is one of the mildest countries in Europe and offers year-round sunshine, making it an ideal destination for a holiday break.

Surrounded west by the Atlantic, south by the Mediterranean and north and east by Spain, the climate is firmly connected with the altitude and proximity to the ocean. Therefore, depending on the region and time of the year, there might be significant variances in the temperature.

While the Atlantic creates a balancing effect on land temperatures, promoting milder summers and winters down the coastline, the Mountains are responsible for colder, wetter conditions in the northern and interior regions. As far as we go down to the Alentejo and the Algarve, the Mediterranean influences get stronger, and summers tend to be longer, dryer, and hotter.

The peak time to explore the Continent is sited between May and mid-October, with average temperatures of 28°C (82°F) in Summer and 21°C (70°F) in Spring.

Regarding the islands, Madeira has a pleasant, sub-tropical climate, with an average temperature of 19°C (66°F), making it a great place to visit at any time. As far as the Azores is concerned, despite the temperature similarity with Madeira, its northwestern location promotes windier and wetter winters. The minimum temperatures at the Azores Archipelago rarely drop under 14°C (57°F) (February is the coldest month), and the maximum temperatures can reach the 24°C (75°F) in August.

MONTH	MIN. AVG. TEMP. (°C)	MAX. AVG. TEMP. (°C)	PRECIPITATION (MM)	RAINY DAYS (LISBOA)
January	4.5	13.1	143.5	14
February	5.6	14.6	117.2	10
March	6.8	17.0	111.3	14
April	8.1	18.2	92.1	10
May	10.5	21.0	60.1	9
June	13.5	25.4	30.5	5
July	15.6	28.7	10.5	2
August	15.5	28.8	13.1	2
September	14.2	26.3	33.7	6
October	11.2	21.2	105.7	9
November	7.9	16.8	134.3	13
December	6.1	13.9	150.0	14
Average	10.0	20.4	83.5	9.0

15

SAFETY

According to the Global Peace Index and the Global Terrorism Index (2017), Portugal is the 3rd safest country in the World, with a distinction of *no impact of terrorism*. Nevertheless, and despite this excellence badge, there are some hazard zones to be avoided by tourists. The main rule is to never do what you wouldn't do in your home country. So, please be careful about leaving your belongings behind, walking through deserted, dark streets, or withdrawing cash in non-monitored areas.

Usually, the main cities are less secure, but the risky streets and neighborhoods are pointed out in the correspondent city/region section, so you can get around them.

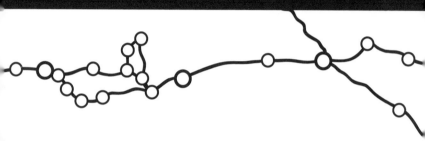

ROAD CONNECTIONS AND CAR RENTING

Portugal's network of highways is an expanding system, with excellent connections across the country. The main roads are generally in good condition and are structured in EN roads (national roads), which establishes a link among the main cities, and IP roads (main itinerary roads), often used as an escape to avoid motorway tolls. As the velocity practiced in EN cannot surpass 90km/hour and the IPs are used as an alternative, traffic jams tend to be more dense and slow. Nevertheless, they are a great way to appreciate the natural Portuguese landscapes and get to know the country.

Another travel option is the motorways (A), where the speed can go up to 120km/hour, definitely accelerating your journey. Please note that most of the Portuguese highways are equipped with tolls, considered a bit expensive, and require a specific electronic tag for the payment. Many car-rental agencies hire out those tags and we strongly recommend confirming its availability before renting a car. If you do not use the device and go through a toll, the probability of receiving a fine (via your car-hire agency) is very high.

To rent a car in Portugal, you must comply with driving license and age requirements. The conditions differ between companies, but the age range is defined between 23 and 25 years old.

Sometimes, a premium payment is applied to inexperienced drivers. Although there are a vast number of rental companies spread across the country, the best rates are often offered online with pre-bookings. Booking a few days in advance is strongly recommended.

Regarding this matter, it is also important to note that most rent-a-car vehicles are equipped with a manual gearbox.

DRIVING ADVICE

Always carry your personal documents with you. If you are stopped by the police, the following papers must be presented: personal ID or passport, driving license, car insurance, rental contract or registration certificate. By law, you should also have a red warning triangle and a fluorescent yellow jacket inside the vehicle, provided by the rental company. Failure to present these documents and objects will incur a fine. Do not try to justify yourself by pleading ignorance. Patience and courtesy will be appreciated.

When planning big trips, fill up the tank with gasoline/diesel (depending on the car specifications) before setting off. Not only can the prices be inflated in motorway gas stations, but it may be hard to find them in remote areas.

When parking the car in big cities, never leave your belongings in sight. It is quite common to find opportunistic people in parking areas, guiding you into a parking space you have just located for yourself, and requesting payment for this service. It is reasonable and wise to hand over some change (at least €0.20) to keep your car safe from scratches.

INTERNET ACCESS

Compared to other European countries, Portugal is definitely a pioneer in internet access infrastructure investment, ensuring great web-connectivity in the Lusitanian Lands. According to a study conducted by *Speedtest* in 2017, the fixed internet access in Portugal ranks in 29th place among the countries best positioned worldwide. It is no coincidence that most public areas offer internet access points at no additional cost to the users.

If you are looking for a hot spot, just go into a coffee shop, a library, or a shopping mall. If wi-fi is not available for open access just look around and see if a password is posted somewhere. If there isn't, you just have to request it at the bar counter or information desk.

Regarding 4G connectivity, the national coverage is over 90%, allowing high-speed internet for any compatible smartphone.

COST OF LIVING

Although prices have gone up in the past years, the currently fashionable Portugal still presents a low cost of living compared to most European Union countries.

From housing to food, transport, and cultural activities, you will find various affordable solutions that will help you control your budget, without sacrificing the thrilling experiences Portugal has to offer.

Accommodation prices are very reasonable and it is quite common to find double rooms in the big cities for 60€/night during the low season.

As may be expected, low-priced products can be found in supermarkets and convenience stores. The established prices for these commercial areas tend to be consistent despite the region. As for meals, restaurants should be considered more expensive, with an average price rating of 15€ to 30€ per person.

A few references:

Coffee – 0,70€
Water bottle – 1,00€
Soda/Beer – 1,30€
Desserts – 4,00€

Note that all the referred prices may vary according to the price rating defined for each region. The price rating compares the cost of living of the different Portuguese cities with the capital (Lisboa) as the maximum reference. It ranks 28th as the most expensive city in Europe (Economist Intelligence Unit, 2017).

TIPS & IDEAS

PORTUGAL VS. SPAIN

It is quite common for non-European citizens to erroneously believe that Portugal is part of the Spanish territory. The truth is that deep inside we get a bit offended by this statement and for most of us it is, in fact, easier to speak English than Spanish.

WALKING AROUND

While wandering around charismatic Portugal, remember that every city holds a tourist office, expert in understanding and exploring the suburban areas, and monuments mentioned in the interactive maps.

Do not forget to search for all the information needed before starting an activity so that you can make the ultimate adventure out of it.

As far as pedestrian trails are concerned, we would strongly advise you not to take them on your own, especially those located in the heart of the mountains. It is quite easy for you to get lost or take the wrong direction.

WATER

Being thirsty in Portugal is not a problem since, as in most European countries, the tap water is safe to drink. The excellent quality of the water for human consumption is corroborated by a safety rate of 99%, according to the Ersar Annual Report, 2016.
Even so, if you are not fond of tap water, the bottled mineral water is of high quality, and the prices are totally affordable.

PURCHASE AND SERVICES

Do not be surprised if people are dispersed in the supermarket areas or public services instead of lining up. In most places, a ticket needs to be issued in advance for you to be served. If you are not sure which option to choose, go for *Geral* (general), from there someone will guide you through the process.

It is also important to underline that since 2015, plastic bags available in the supermarkets, pharmacies, or bookshops are taxed 0,10€ or more each as a measure to protect and preserve the environment.

BARGAINING

Haggling in Portugal is not usual, although a gentle bargain is accepted in specific shopping locations such as open-air markets and handicraft markets. Be aware that some merchants might try to take advantage of tourists, overpricing the products they are selling.

Notwithstanding, you won't experience this issue often; most sellers are trustworthy.

The stated price is expected to be paid in any other circumstance.

ETIQUETTE

• Shake hands when greeting someone. A family atmosphere invites you (either male or female) to greet women with two kisses.

• Men are expected to take off their hats in indoor spaces.

• Women should cover their shoulders inside religious monuments.

• Offer your seat to the elderly or to a pregnant woman in public transportation.

• Be patient. The Portuguese tend to arrive late everywhere except important meetings. If dinner is scheduled for 7.30pm, it is likely to begin an hour later.

• Try not to feel uncomfortable if people stand close to you in a conversation. Proximity is not a big deal to the Portuguese.

• It is common for people touch your arm or hand during a conversation. The sense of proximity is deeply rooted in the Portuguese culture.

• Pointing fingers at people or staring at them is considered disrespectful.

• Eating with your fingers is a sign of rudeness.

• Try not to munch, slurp or burp while eating. The Portuguese are not very fond of table noises.

• Speaking loudly or cursing in public is a sign of bad manners and low social status.

• Do not spit on the floor, this is reprehensible and disrespectful behavior.

SMOKING

If you are a smoker, be aware that smoking in public closed areas is not allowed, unless the facility is equipped with the necessary ventilation system. Today it is quite common to find a physical division in coffee shops or restaurants for smokers and non-smokers. Just make sure you respect this conduct regulation.

HOMOSEXUALITY

90% of the Portuguese follow the Roman Catholic Church, which translates into conservatism. Although most people accept same-sex relationships, the region where you are will change the level of acceptance. This acceptance has increased substantially in Porto, Lisboa, and Algarve in the past few years, but you should expect some raised eyebrows in other small regions. A discreet profile is recommended.

PORTUGUESE LANGUAGE SURVIVAL KIT

One of the first noticeable things about the Portuguese people is that they communicate and comprehend the English language very well. So, it is quite easy for a tourist to get instructions and directions in the bigger cities, mainly from the younger generation. However, as you go deeper into the country, it may be necessary for you to use some of our expressions to be understood. For this purpose, we arranged a Portuguese survival kit:

	ENGLISH	PORTUGUESE
1.	Hello	Olá
2.	Goodbye	Adeus / tchau
3.	Do you speak English?	Fala inglês?
4.	I don't speak portuguese	Não falo português
5.	Yes	Sim
6.	No	Não
7.	Food	Comida
8.	Beverage	Bebida
9.	Please	Por favor
10.	Restroom	Casa de banho
11.	Excuse me	Com licença
12.	See you later	Até logo
13.	Where is...	Onde fica...
14.	I want...	Quero...
15.	I need to...	Preciso de...
16.	Sorry (call for attention)	Desculpe
17.	Everything's ok?	Tudo bem?
18.	Congratulations	Parabéns

If even after the explanation you are still having trouble, as a last resort, try to utilize hand gestures. A real local will go the extra mile to catch you up.

EVENT
GUIDE

JANUARY	Aveiro	St. *Gonçalinho* Festival

FEBRUARY	Porto	*Fantasporto* Porto International Film Festival
	Bragança	*Butelo* and *Casulas* Festival
	Guarda	*Guardafolia* Carnival parade
	Torres Vedras	Carnival parade
	Beja	*Terras sem Sombra* sacred music Festival
	Funchal	Carnival Festivities

MARCH	Aveiro	*Feira de Março*
	Portalegre	*Jazzfest* – Jazz Festival
	Lisboa	Lisboa Fashion Week
	Setúbal	*St. José* Festival (Municipal Holiday)

APRIL	National Holiday	25th April – Liberation Day
	Portalegre	Conventual sweets' Fair
	Lisboa	*Lisboa Fish & Flavours*, food festival
		Estoril Open, ATP World Tour – Estoril
	Beja	*Obiveja* Agricultural Fair
	Funchal	Flower Festival
	São Miguel Island	*Senhor Santo Cristo dos Milagres* Festival
	Madeira Archipelago	*Espírito Santo* Festival (until September)

MAY	Braga	*Braga Romana*
	Bragança	*Cantarinhas* Market
		Handicraft Fair
	Aveiro	*St. Joana, the Princess* Festival (Municipal Holiday)
	Castelo Branco	Templar days (Beginning of June)

EVENT GUIDE

Leiria	City Day
	May Fair
Portalegre	*The Aprons* Festival
	City Festival (Municipal Holiday)
Lisboa	*Rock in Rio* Festival (biannual)
Alcântara, Lisboa	*Alkantara* Festival
Fátima, Santarém	Religious Celebrations
Beja	*Dia da Espiga* – Corn cob day (Municipal Holiday)
	International Comics' Festival (late May, early June)

JUNE	National Holiday	10th June – National Day
	Viana do Castelo	Medieval Fair
	Braga	*St. João* Festival (Municipal Holiday)
	Vila Real	*St. António* Festival (Municipal Holiday)
		Rock *Nordeste* Summer Festival
		WTCC – FIA World Touring Car Championship
	Porto	*Serralves* Festival
		St. João Festival (Municipal Holiday)
	Viseu	*Cavalhadas de Vildemoinhos*
	Coimbra	Medieval Fair
		Popular Fair
	Lisboa	*St. António* Festival (Municipal Holiday)
	Santarém	National Agricultural Fair
	Évora	*St. João* Fair
		St. Peter's Day (Municipal Holiday)
	Funchal, Madeira	*Atlantic* Festival
	Terceira, Açores	*Sanjoaninas* Festival

JULY	Matosinhos, Porto	*Meo Marés Vivas* Summer Festival
	Guarda	City Festivities
	Coimbra	*St. Isabel* Festival, even years (Municipal Holiday)
		Arts Festival
	Torres Vedras, Lisboa	*Santa Cruz* Ocean Spirit – Surf Competition
	Óbidos, Leiria	*Óbidos* Medieval Fair
	Lisboa	*Super Bock Super Rock* Music Festival
		NOS Alive Music Festival
	Setúbal	*Sant'Iago* Fair
	Ria Formosa, Faro	*Ria Formosa* Festival

AUGUST	Viana do Castelo	*Nossa Senhora d'Agonia* Religious Festival
		Neo Pop Summer Festival
		Vilar de Mouros Festival
	Bragança	*Festa da História* – Medieval Fair
		Nossa Senhora das Graças Festival (Municipal Holiday)
	Ílhavo, Aveiro	*Ílhavo Codfish* Festival
	Viseu	*São Mateus* Fair, handicraft fair
	Coimbra	*Feira das Cebolas*, Onions' Fair
	Leiria	*Entremuralhas* Summer Festival
	Setúbal	*Marisco no Largo* Food Festival
	Zambujeira, Beja	*Zambujeira do Mar Meo Sudoeste* Music Festival
	Faro	*FolkFaro* – International Folclore Festival
	Silves, Faro	*Silves* Medieval Fair
	Faro	*F* Festival – Art and Culture Festival
	Funchal, Madeira	*Madeira* Wine Festival
	Pico Island, Açores	*Senhor Bom Jesus Milagroso* Festival
	Corvo Island, Açores	*Senhora dos Milagres* Festival
	Pico Island, Azores	*Senhor Bom Jesus Milagroso* Festival
	Faial Island, Azores	*Senhora da Guia* Festival

EVENT GUIDE

SEPTEMBER	Ponte de Lima, Viana do Castelo	*Feiras Novas* Traditional Fair
	Braga	White Night
	Porto	*Noites Ritual* Summer Festival
	Viseu	*St. Mateus* Festival (Municipal Holiday)
	Guarda	*Feira Farta*, local products fair
	Portalegre	*Feira das Cebolas*, Onions' Fair
	Seixal, Setúbal	*Avante* Festival in Atalaia
	Palmela, Setúbal	*The Grape Harvest* Festival
	Setúbal	*Bocage* and City Day
	Faro	City Day (Municipal Holiday)
	Porto Santo Island, Madeira	*Columbus* Festival

OCTOBER	National Holiday	5th October – Republic Day
	Portalegre	*Baja 500* Portalegre, FIA championship
	Lisboa	Lisboa Fashion Week
	Santarém	National Gastronomy Festival
	Beja	*RuralBeja* Festival
	Santa Iria, Faro	*Santa Iria* Fair
	Madeira	*Nature* Festival Week

NOVEMBER	Vila Real	FAG – Handicrafts and Gastronomy Fair
	Guarda	Municipal Holiday
	Golegã, Santarém	*Golegã Equestrian* Fair
	Borba, Évora	*Borba Vineyard and Wine* Festival

DECEMBER	National Holiday	1st December – Ind. Restoration Day
	Leça da Palmeira, Porto	*Comic Con* Portugal
	Guarda	Guarda: City of Christmas
	Funchal, Madeira	New Year Festivities

ACCOMMODATION

Portugal offers a wide range of accommodation options for tourists all over the country. Please find below a general explanation:

ACCOMMODATION TYPES

HOTEL	POUSADAS DE PORTUGAL	HOSTEL	ESTALAGEM / INN
Classified from 1 to 5 stars according to the comfort, luxury, and services provided	Hotel facilities in country's most historical and iconic buildings (Castles, Palaces, Monasteries)	Accommodation services in individual or collective rooms, priced below the regular hotel	Family-run small hotel/lodge, modest in size and at affordable prices

Hotels and *Pousadas de Portugal* are highly acclaimed internationally for their comfort, facilities, and food services. They generally stand out for the hospitability and the professionalism of the staff and delicious American and European breakfasts. The high quality of the 4 and 5 stars Portuguese hotels is well-renowned in excellence when compared with other European hotels with the same rating.

For reduced rates, you will effortlessly find other alternatives, such as youth hostels or camping facilities. A pre-booking is needed for Hotels, *Pousadas de Portugal*, and Hostels. Some of them may also require the payment made upfront by credit card. As for the *Estalagens* / Inns, youth hostels, and camping facilities usually the payment is on-site.

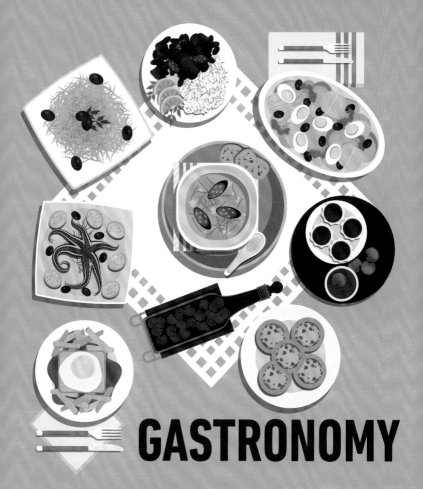

GASTRONOMY

Portuguese cuisine has everything to please even the most demanding gourmand. Deeply rooted in the fresh local ingredients and based on genuine quality products, it provides a burst of complex flavors and delightfulness. The traditional recipes aligned with the most innovative and unusual trends make the national gastronomy a closely guarded secret for foreigners. Nevertheless, the successful chefs are crossing borders, and more and more enthusiasts are coming to understand this utterly delicious food culture.

The Portuguese connection with the Ocean is enormous and the fishermen live in perfect unison with the Atlantic, bringing to land the best fish in the entire world. Together with the fresh fish, shellfish also reach the top-quality restaurants in Europe and America every day, to customers' delight.

The legendary Port wine is another international icon from Portugal, known for its unique characteristics of sumptuousness and sensuality. However, it is not the only astonishing wine produced in Lusitanian Lands. As you cross the country, you will be surprised with green, full-bodied and even bubbly wines harvested from picturesque vineyards.

Many sinful Portuguese pastries were originally baked in convents, as the nuns needed a supplement to their incomes. We literally should thank God for the heavenly *Pastel de Nata* and its pure evil alternatives.

Fresh fruits and vegetables are often on the table, as they add a distinctive and healthy taste to the dishes and soups – a common comfort-food before any main dish. Our new organic production methods can be confirmed in every town market across the country, as you enjoy a daily show of freshness and natural scents.

Other distinguished products are the succulent Protected Denomination of Origin (*DOP*) meats, tasty cheeses, and pure aromatic olive oils. Any of these marvelous delicacies go perfectly with a bite of delicious bread.

GASTRONOMIC SPECIALTIES BY REGION

PORTO AND THE NORTH	• *Alheira*: smoked chorizo pork free • *Bola de Lamego*: baked loaf stuffed with meats • *Broa de Avintes*: cornbread • *Cabrito*: roasted kid • *Caldo Verde*: kale and chorizo soup • *Enchidos*: smoked sausage • *Francesinha*: sandwich of stake or roast meat and smoked sausages covered with melted cheese • *Port Wine*: full-bodied red wine from the Douro region • *Posta Mirandesa*: DOP cattle meat • *Rojões*: braised pork chunks • *Sarrabulho*: pork rice cooked in pig blood • *Tripas à moda do Porto*: tripe with haricot beans • *Vinho Verde*: summery wine from the green northwest
CENTER	• *Azeite da Beira Baixa*: olive oil • *Bacalhau*: salt cod • *Caldeirada*: fish stew • *Castanhas de ovos*: conventual pastry of raw egg yolk and sugar syrup • *Cerejas*: cherries • *Chanfana de cabra*: goat casserole cooked slowly in red wine • *Leitão da Bairrada*: roast suckling pig • *Mel*: honey • *Ovos moles*: communion wafers filled with raw egg yolk and sugar syrup • *Pão-de-Ló de Ovar*: traditional sponge cake • *Pastéis de Tentúgal*: puff pastry filled with raw egg yolk and sugar syrup • *Queijo da Serra*: semi-soft and buttery cheese • *Vitela*: roast veal

LISBOA AND THE TAGUS VALLEY	• *Choco frito*: fried cuttlefish • *Caldeirada*: fish stew • *Moscatel de Setúbal*: muscatel • *Nozes*: walnuts • *Pampilhos*: shortcrust pastry filled with raw egg yolk, sugar syrup, and cinnamon • *Pastéis de Belém/Nata*: custard tart • *Queijadas*: cheese tarts • *Queijo de Azeitão*: feta cheese • *Salmonete de Setúbal*: red mullet • *Sardinha assada*: grilled sardines • *Tortas de Azeitão*: egg cream-filled rolls • *Travesseiros*: egg and almond pastries • *Vinhos da Adega do Cartaxo*: Adega do Cartaxo table wines
SOUTH	• *Açorda de marisco*: seafood bread casserole • *Açorda*: Alentejo soup-like dish made with bread, eggs and herbs including coriander • *Aguardente de medronho*: traditional fruit brandy • *Alfarroba*: carob • *Amêndoas*: almonds • *Arroz de lingueirão*: razor clam rice • *Carapaus alimados*: skinned horse mackerel • *Carne de porco à alentejana*: fried pork meat with clams and fried potatoes • *Carne de porco frita*: fried pork meat • *Cozido de grão*: boiled meats and chickpeas • *Estupeta de atum*: tuna steak • *Feijoada de búzios*: whelk bean stew • *Figos*: figs • *Galinha cerejada*: braised chicken • *Laranja*: oranges • *Licor de amêndoa amarga*: bitter almond liqueur • *Maçapão*: marzipan – hard almond paste cakes • *Marisco*: seafood – clams, oysters, donax clams and cockles • *Migas*: Alentejo bread soup • *Morgados*: small cakes made with sugar, almond, eggs, angel hair and pumpkin • *Pastéis de Santa Clara*: egg and almond pastries • *Percebes*: barnacles • *Polvo, lulas e chocos*: octopus, squid and cuttlefish • *Queijadas*: cheese tarts • *Queijos de ovelha e de cabra*: sheep and goat cheese, dry, half cured or creamy • *Sericaia*: combination of eggs, milk, sugar and cinnamon • *Sopa de gaspacho*: gazpacho soup • *Toucinho-do-céu*: sugar and egg yolk sweet • *Trouxas-de-ovos*: sugar and yolk-based "egg bundles" • *Vinho do Alentejo*: red wines – Portalegre, Borba, Redondo, Reguengos, Vidigueira ou Moura • *Xerém de conquilhas*: clam stew with maize meal

- Alcatra: fish or beef casserole
- Ananás: pineapple
- Atum: tuna
- Bolo de mel: honey cake
- Bolo do caco: bread baked on a piece of tile which usually accompanies kebabs with garlic butter
- Bolo lêvedo: leavened cake
- Carne de vinha-d'alhos: wine and garlic marinated beef
- Cozido das Furnas: mix of stewed pork, beef and chicken with vegetables and enchidos
- Cuscuz caseiro: home-made couscous
- Espetada de vaca em pau de loureiro: beef kebab on a bay stick
- Filetes de peixe-espada preto: black scabbard fish fillets
- Frutos tropicais: tropical fruits – banana, passion fruit, mango, cherimoya
- Inhames com linguiça: yam with sausage
- Licores de maracuja e ananás: passion fruit and pineapple liqueurs
- Marisco: seafood – limpets, barnacles and locust lobsters
- Massa sovada: sweet bread
- Mel: honey
- Milho frito: crunchy fried corn
- Polvo: octopus stewed in aromatic wine
- Poncha da Madeira: brandy prepared with honey and lemon
- Queijadas de Vila Franca do Campo: cheese tarts
- Queijo de S. Jorge: cow's milk and salt cheese with a spicy flavor
- Rosquilhas de batata-doce: ring-shaped yam loaves
- Sopa de trigo: wheat soup
- Vinhos regionais: regional wines – Sercial, Boal, Verdelho and Malvasia

TASCAS

To describe a *Tasca* can be tricky, for you must feel it and smell it to understand its essence. A standard definition could be a place where a glass of wine and something else to crack are kings. These small, cheap, and familiar environments are gathering spots for groups of friends seeking to socialize and have a good time. A *Tasca* or Tavern (closest English word) is also responsible for introducing foreigners to real hearty Portuguese cuisine.

In each section/region of this travel guide, you will be able to meet some of the most traditional *Tascas* and taste its delicious delicacies.

Here are some examples of the savory tidbits or tapas you will find:

- *Bolinhos de bacalhau* (codfish cakes)
- *Pataniscas* (codfish tempuras)
- *Croquettes*
- *Rojões* (braised pork chunks)
- *Moelas* (gizzards)

- *Orelheira* (pigs' ear salad)
- *Tripas* (browned tripe)
- *Bifana* (pork steak sandwich)
- *Caracóis* (escargots)
- *Cogumelos* (mushrooms)
- *Polvo* (octopus salad)
- *Caldo verde* (kale and chorizo soup)
- Chorizos, ham and cheese
- *Tremoços* (lupin beans)
- Olives
- Peanuts and salty snacks
- Wine
- Bottled or draft beer

Note that depending on the Region and on the house specialty, the tidbits may vary. Don't just read about them, hit the road and discover these superb feasts.

PS: do not pay regular visits to Tascas. Although the food is absolutely amazing, your health may not enjoy it as much as you do.

COFFEE SHOPS AND PATISSERIES

Coffee and sugar, what a blessing from the Age of Discovery! The Portuguese audacity in combining these two ingredients, aligned with the nuns' magic touch, transformed our breakfasts into pure ambrosia.

If you are looking for the perfect spot to taste an authentic morning meal, Coffee shops and Patisseries are the places to go. You are likely to find one on every street corner with appealing pastry and bread storefronts. Sometimes the pleasant smell emanating from the buildings is hard to resist and mouth-watering is inevitable. But it's not only the pastries and the bread, the real issue is when you combine them with coffee or milk. That is something that you absolutely cannot miss.

Aside from breakfast, some of these places also serve light meals for lunch and snacks. Usually, they are cheaper than restaurants and the service is faster. So, if you are in a hurry to check all the items on your bucket list, a Coffee shop or a Patisserie can be an excellent option.

The first thing to know before you go is that some restaurants demand a reservation, especially those close to the metropolis. Calling beforehand is the ideal scenario since most of the restaurants do not use technological reservation platforms such as "The Fork." The pre-reservation will also help you to understand the opening hours. Meals are usually served from 12pm to 3pm and from 7pm to 10pm. However, some places located in touristic areas can practice different schedules.

It is quite easy to develop empathy with the waitstaff in Portugal. These hospitality professionals are trained to serve you the best way possible, but when it comes to smaller commercial businesses, the English language can become a bit rudimentary. After smoothly overcoming this initial hurdle with a few hand gestures, it's time for the first cultural shock. Do not feel upset if the waiter does not come back to check on you after getting your order. To be noticed, just raise your hand, saying "por favor" or "please". This cultural detail is common in most of the places unless you are in an expensive restaurant.

As soon as you seat at the table, a range of starters/appetizers will fly down on you. Be aware that these unordered pâtés, bread, olives, cheese, butter (etc.) are not for free. If you want to save yourself for the main dish, a gentle "no thank you" will save you some money. Also note that they are not allowed to charge you the goodies if you just let them sit on the table, untouched.

When placing your order, you will face a quantity challenge. As you read the menu, develop the ability to understand that 1 dose is meant for 2 people and ½ a dose serves one perfectly. Don't make the mistake of ordering 1 dose for one, you will waste not only a lot of food but also money.

As you leave the restaurant, do not feel any obligation to tip the waitstaff as they will appreciate it, but it is not mandatory nor rude not to tip. These professionals are paid a standard wage and do not rely on tips as the Americans or Mexicans do. Rounding off a bill to the nearest euro is generous enough.

SERVICE

ID, PASSPORT AND VISA

Portugal is a very friendly Nation when it comes to relations with the rest of the World. If you are coming from a member state of the Schengen Area, your ID/Passport allows you to cross the border and travel freely inside the country for 90 days. The same applies to citizens whose countries signed agreements/treaties with Portugal.

Before leaving, please confirm if your country is on the following list: https://foxhoundglobal.com/yourls/visacountries – if so you are required to have a visa to visit Portugal and should contact the nearest Portuguese Embassy in advance.

USEFUL CONTACTS

SERVICE	CONTACT
Emergency	112
Fire Department	117
Health 24 (health support by telephone)	+351 808 24 24 24
Maritime Search and Rescue	+351 214 401 919
Intoxication line	+351 808 250 143
CP (train info)	+351 707 210 220
Rede Expressos (bus info)	+351 707 223 344

HEALTH INSURANCE

Coming from one of the 28 European Union Members, Iceland, Liechtenstein, Norway, or Switzerland? If the answer is positive, the European Health Insurance Card gives you access to the Portuguese health system as a national and you are totally protected, regarding medical care.

If you are coming from a non-European State, private health insurance should be arranged. This type of coverage assures your access to public and private hospitals and clinics and the treatments detailed in your contract.

Please note that the lack of insurance puts you in a very fragile position and a simple broken leg can be very expensive.

As far as Pharmacies are concerned, the regular opening hours are positioned between 9 am and 8 pm. To check the on-duty pharmacy (24 hours) in your area, please check the *Farmácias Portuguesas* App.

CURRENCY

Portugal is an active Member State in the European Economic Monetary Union and in 2002 the Euro (€) became its official currency. Currently, Europeans from 19 countries use the Euro every day, being the second most-used currency in the world.

Banks and agencies registered within the *Banco de Portugal* are the best places to exchange your local currency to Euros. Nevertheless, bear in mind that these financial entities are not obliged to do it.

Please find below some useful official links to guide you through the process:

AUTHORIZED EXCHANGE INSTITUTIONS

UP-TO-DATE EXCHANGE RATES

CURRENCY CONVERTER

The Portuguese financial technology is considered one of the best in Europe, so you can easily pay with your credit or debit card in a supermarket, store, hotel, or restaurant. On the other hand, if you need cash, ATM machines are a simple way to get it and are not difficult to find in the cities. The daily withdraw permitted amount is 400€ (200€ + 200€), and the fees are around 2% or 3%, depending on the bank (refer to *How to read* section for saving fees options). If you are planning to travel to rural villages, cash in advance could be a wise solution, since not all of them are equipped with ATMs.

TRANSPORTATION

Portugal is a well-served country as far as public transportation is concerned, nonetheless the connections are better and faster between the big cities, as can be expected. As for the rest of the national territory, we would like to share some recommendations and useful information:

BUS

Rede-Expressos offers innumerous bus connections from North to South. Schedules and bus stops are available at www.rede-expressos.pt/en/.

For local connections, please refer to the City Transportation section available in each capital of the district.

PORTO CENTRAL STATION	LISBOA CENTRAL STATION
Terminal Rodoviário Campo 24 de Agosto, 1254 300-504 Porto Metro station: 24 de Agosto	Praça Marechal Humberto Delgado, Sete Rios 1500 Lisboa Metro station: Jardim Zoológico

TRAINS

CP – *Comboios de Portugal* is the only railway company in the country. Trains are categorized as follows:

***Urbanos* (U):** operate inside Porto, Lisboa, and Coimbra;

***Regional* (R):** local service stopping at all stations;

***InterRegional* (IR):** medium distance service linking the more important villages and towns;

***Intercidades* (IC):** long distance service connecting the main cities;

***Alfa Pendular* (AP):** high speed train linking the major Portuguese cities.

Schedules and stops are available at www.cp.pt/passageiros/en.

PORTO MAIN STATIONS
• Campanhã
• São Bento
Metro stations: same name as above

LISBOA MAIN STATIONS
• Oriente
• Santa Apolónia
Metro stations: same name as above

AIRPORTS

For your reference, Portugal houses six international airports, all connected by TAP Air Portugal. Most of them are also served by low-cost companies such as Ryanair or EasyJet:

• *Humberto Delgado Airport*, Lisboa (LIS)
• *Francisco Sá Carneiro*, Porto (OPO)
• *Cristiano Ronaldo Airport*, Funchal – Madeira (FNC)
• *Faro Airport*, Algarve (FAO)
• *João Paulo II Airport*, Ponta Delgada – Açores (PDL)
• *Lajes*, Terceira – Açores (TER)

Apart from the international airports previously mentioned, there are also secondary airports and aerodromes that allow commercial connections among the Islands or other regions of the country.

HOW TO READ

Looking to promote a practical and user-friendly Travel Guide, a variety of features were included in this publication. Apart from the original and playful bucket list, the Travel Guide is also endowed with mobile integration and QR Codes to facilitate the interaction between users and the explanatory remarks present along the guide.

These two functionalities not only put aside the old-fashioned and inconvenient maps, but also enable travelers to exploit interactive ones, taking an active part in the journey.

Moving quickly between the Travel Guide's theoretical information and cellular phones can be easily done in this first edition, adapted to eBook and paper version.

A Brief description of the district and its distinctive characteristics:

DID YOU KNOW THAT

A historical or cultural curiosity that gets you into the spirit of the region and works as a conversation trigger with the locals.

7 PLACES TO VISIT*

The 7 most emblematic cultural landmarks of the region and a short overview of its usability or representativeness.

3 PLACES TO EAT + 1 *TASCA*

More than indicating the best places, the main objective is to translate the region's gastronomy and show the dishes' and prices' diversity. The dominant food type was included, together with a simplified price range whereby the one € symbol is equivalent to affordable food, and the three €€€ represents higher costs associated.

3 PLACES TO SLEEP*

Diversity and proximity are both taken into account in this category. Apart from the star rating, previously explained in the *Accommodation* section, the distance between the district capital and the accommodation venue is also considered.

Each recommendation has a QR Code associated that redirects you straight to its *booking.com* page. If you have the Booking app installed, it will be automatically opened when you scan the QRCode with your mobile device camera.

SPECIAL DATES

Even though there's a glimpse of the commemorative dates per month in the *Event Guide* section, we chose to divide the information per region, so the travelers could better plan their journeys.

BUCKET LIST*

The must-do adventures for every region. The

game component is explored to the maximum so activities could be more engaging and challenging. The bucket list can also include visits to secondary sites, located outside the district capital. It is up to the traveler to decide to take the detour. A checkbox is also available to control the number of performed activities, and our travel guide team is eager for feedback.

CITY TRANSPORTATION
Benchmark transportation companies in the region with direct links to general information, schedules, and tickets.

HOW TO GET TO
A brief explanation of how to get to the city center by car, train, bus or metro (if applicable).

AREAS TO AVOID
In past years, some neighborhoods have been identified as problematic, and concerns have risen. Although most of these areas are now being requalified and improvement is expected in the interim, it is important not to cross them alone, especially at night.

PRICE RATING
According to the Portuguese cost of living, a scale rating was organized whereby the Capital (Lisboa) is considered the maximum reference (€€€€€). Nevertheless, it is important to highlight that a price variety usually applies to the touristic regions, mainly in the summer months (June, July, and August).

SHOPPING
Shopping reference areas in each capital of the district, including traditional commercial streets and shopping centers.

*Particular attention was given to Porto and Lisboa cities due to its cultural richness and dimension. An in-depth analysis was taken and extra care was added to widen the regions' information and activities.

USEFUL APPS

If you're using Android, you'll have to install *Lightning QR Scanner* to use your phone's camera to read the information, either a map, phone number or web link. On iPhone/iPad, just point the phone camera at the code, you'll get a pop-up with the respectively associated action.

To read our custom maps with points of interest and to navigate between them, use *Google Maps*. Before traveling, we suggest you download the offline version of the Portuguese map so you won't need to use mobile data.

If hand gestures aren't working, you should have a B plan. *iTranslate* will allow you to translate most languages to Portuguese, enabling the phone to talk on your behalf. The premium version allows offline translation, which might be helpful to avoid mobile data charges.

Want to have up-to-date exchange rates? Install *XE Currency*, and you'll quickly calculate the amount in Euros.

Although Google Maps includes turn-by-turn navigation, we find *Meo Drive* quite appealing (and free). It allows you to download the map to avoid mobile data charges.

Most banks will charge you up to 10% in withdrawal/transfer fees. *Revolut* is a digital bank that includes a pre-paid debit card and currency exchange, so you pay almost nothing for using Euros.

When it comes to distances and weights, we've used the International System of Units, which is also the Portuguese one. To easily convert them to imperial/US units, *Unit Converter* is quite handy.

We've included all district hospitals on the map. If you need medicine, there is always a 24h pharmacy open in every city. To know which one is available, install *Farmácias Portuguesas*. It provides an English translation.

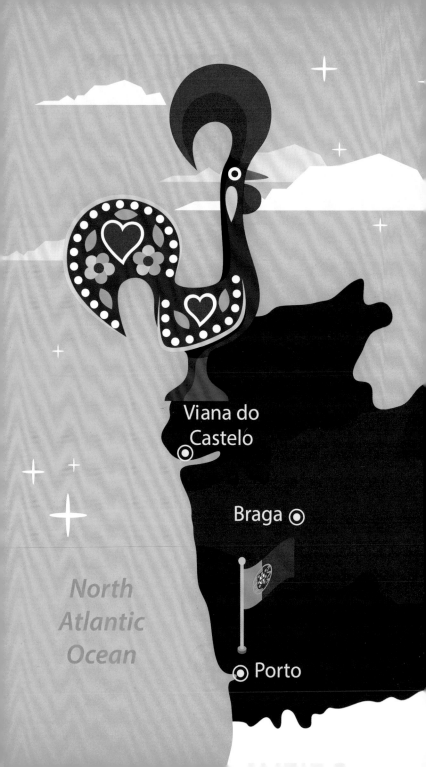

Viana do Castelo

Braga

North
Atlantic
Ocean

Porto

PORTO AND THE NORTH

Bragança ◉

Vila Real

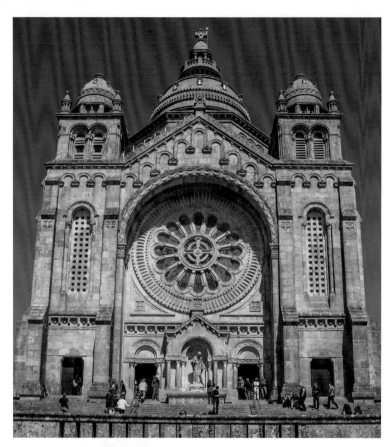

VIANA DO CASTELO

This northern city of Minho Region has definitely one of the most breathtaking landscapes in Portugal. You just have to get the funicular straight to Santa Luzia Monastery to dive into the heart of Viana do Castelo. Surrounded by green mountains, where Lima river flows and bathed by the deep blue of the Atlantic Ocean its involving and colorful traditions will make you fall in love.

DID YOU KNOW THAT...

There was a huge castle in the area and people usually stopped by just to stare its greatness. Occasionally, this stunning princess (rosy cheeks, light eyes, and long blond hair), named Ana, looked through the window for the villagers' astonishment. As she was timid, every time she foresaw someone's footsteps on the street she would hide. It was then very rare and a privilege to see her. Those who did, ran telling: "I saw Ana at the Castle" (eu *Vi Ana no Castelo*).
And this is where the name of the city comes from – Viana do Castelo.

7 PLACES TO VISIT

1 SANTA LUZIA MONUMENT-TEMPLE
The construction work began in 1904, developing quickly up until the proclamation of Portugal as a republic (1910). With the epoch instability aggravated by the First World War, only in 1959, the Temple was completed entirely. The monument is dedicated to the Santa Luzia and the Sacred Heart of Jesus Christ-devotion.

2 CITADEL OF SANTA LUZIA
Known locally as the "Old Town", it is one of the most famous fortresses in northern Portugal and definitely one of the most important for the study of Proto-history and the *Alto Minho* Romanization.

3 *SANTIAGO DA BARRA* FORTRESS
Built in the 13th century in the reign of King Afonso III, its function was to protect and develop the region, fostering the commercial and fishing activity.

4 *GIL EANNES* HOSPITAL SHIP
The hospital ship assisted for decades the Portuguese codfish fleet in Newfoundland and Greenland. Gil Eannes Foundation recognized it as cultural heritage in 1998 and converted it into a public museum.

5 HISTORICAL FORTRESS OF VALENÇA DO MINHO AND THE CITADEL
Fortified in the 17th century in the style of the French military architect, *Vauban*, Valença is a city with a very flourishing trade. The pieces produced by the local craftsmen are the most sought-after products in the entire region.

6 COSTUME MUSEUM (*MUSEU DO TRAJE*)
Located in the historical center, the Museum shows the audacity and the creativity of the women from the region. It oversees the study, preservation, and diffusion of the cultural heritage.

7 PONTE DE LIMA
The oldest town in Portugal hides deep roots and ancestral legends. The different architectural styles represented in its buildings, streets, and bridge express the tremendous historical and cultural value of this charismatic and ancient town.

47

3 PLACES TO EAT

3 PLACES TO SLEE

TASQUINHA DA LINDA

Seafood
€ €

Tiny restaurant with fresh fish and shellfish. You'll get the very best meal that a fisherman can provide. Make sure you make a reservation!

+351 258 847 900

RESTAURANTE CAMELO

Portuguese
€ €

Traditional and prestigious restaurant with excellent regional food. Nice family environment. Great place to have a typical Portuguese *Sarrabulho*.

+351 258 839 090

SR. BIFE RESTAURANTE

Portuguese
€ €

Its name says it all – "Steak Restaurant". Great location near the river, they serve some genuine Portuguese steaks.

+351 965 319 300

TASCA NECAS VIEIRA

Tasca

Necas is the owner of this establishment that lives to serve others. At this very typical Portuguese *tasca*, you'll find one of the best-stuffed gizzards – *moelas*, to be accompanied by some fine green wine from the region. They also have great smoked ham and trapped eggs – *ovos entalados*.

+351 258 831 643

POUSADA DE VIANA DO CASTELO

★ ★ ★ ★
3KM

Placed on top of the Santa Luzia mountain, this *Pousada de Portugal* provides the best view over the city. Although the room decoration is a bit outdated, everything else compensates it immensely: the location, the premium restaurant, attentive staff, and tranquility.
You can easily take the Funicular to get back to town.

+351 258 800 370
guest@pousadas.pt

QUINTA BOUÇA D'ARQUES

Guesthouse
11KM

Placed in the south part of the *Lima* river it's considered the best place to sleep in Viana do Castelo. This farmhouse merges perfectly into the natural surroundings, being quiet and peaceful. Its owners are super friendly and helpful.

+351 967 571 524
joaomcouto@net.sapo.pt

FÁBRICA DO CHOCOLATE HOTEL

★ ★ ★ ★ ★
1KM

Century-old building, where chocolate used to be produced. It turned into a chocolate-themed hotel and museum. If you love chocolate, it's an interesting place to visit and stay.

+ 351 258 244 000
reservas@fabricadochocolate.com

BUCKET LIST

- [ ] Eat a *Bola de Berlim* at Pastelaria Confeitaria Manuel Natário (pastry)
- [ ] Take a picture with someone wearing the regional costume
- [ ] Taste the city chocolate Avianense at the Chocolate Factory Museum
- [ ] Watch a *Zés P'reiras* Parade (traditional drums)
- [ ] Walk through the city Fair (every Friday at Campo D'Agonia)
- [ ] Find the mini train running at Estação Viana Shopping ceiling
- [ ] Watch a show at Centro Cultural de Viana do Castelo
- [ ] Taste Alvarinho wine
- [ ] Climb Santa Luzia Mount using the Funicular (cable car)
- [ ] Get photographed by the analog camera photographer at Santa Luzia
- [ ] Climb Santa Luzia Cupola (250m above sea level)
- [ ] Try a nautical sport at the *Lima* river
- [ ] Take a walk at Praia Norte beach waterfront
- [ ] Taste the traditional porc dish *Papas de Sarrabulho* (Ponte de Lima)
- [ ] Cross the border to Spain in a Ferry-boat (Caminha)

SPECIAL DATES

- *Medieval* Fair (June)
- *Nossa Senhora d'Agonia* Religious Festival (August 20th – Municipal Holiday)
- *Neo Pop* Summer Festival (August)
- *Paredes de Coura* Festival (August) – Paredes de Coura
- *Vilar de Mouros* Festival (August) – Vilar de Mouros
- *Feiras Novas* Traditional Fair (September) – Ponte de Lima

SHOPPING

- Estação Viana Shopping – Rua General Humberto Delgado, 101
- Rua da Bandeira
- Rua Manuel Espregueira

HOW TO GET TO

🚗 CAR
Porto: 🕐 1h00 🛣 A28
Lisboa: 🕐 4h00 🛣 A1, A28

🚆 TRAIN
Porto: 🕐 1h30 🚉 IR ➡ Viana do Castelo
Lisboa: 🕐 4h30 🚉 AP ➡ Nine ⇄ R ➡ Viana do Castelo

🚌 BUS
Porto: 🕐 1h30
Lisboa: 🕐 4h30

ℹ CITY TRANSPORTATION
Bus: AVIC – www.avic.pt
AV Minho – www.avminho.pt

PRICE RATING

BRAGA

Elegance, history, and spirituality are the best adjectives to describe the third-largest city in the country. Full of vivacity and movement, it was pronounced the European Youth Capital in 2012.

Walking through the city, you will discover the constant bells chiming and its imponent churches and chapels. The living cafes and the fancy boutiques will definitely arouse your passion.

DID YOU KNOW THAT...

Braga is known as the city of priests, who ruled the city for almost seven centuries. Those were the responsible for the urbanistic revolution within it, ripping doors in the Wall, opening and widening the streets, creating large squares and endowing the city with fountains and churches.

7 PLACES TO VISIT

1 BOM JESUS DO MONTE SANCTUARY
Characterized as the symbol of the city, this sober neoclassical catholic sanctuary is dedicated to the Lord of Bom Jesus. The high part of the city is connected to the top of the Mount by a monumental staircase of 17 landings and a cable car – an impressive engineering piece of the 19th century.

2 SAMEIRO SANCTUARY
Situated at 566m above the sea level, Sameiro Sanctuary was gifted with an impressive view over the region. Particular interest is given to its silver tabernacle and a statue of its patron sculped by the Italian Eugénio Maccagnani during the 1880's.

3 MONASTERY OF ST. MARTIM OF TIBÃES
Dated from the 6th century it is the old motherhouse of the Portuguese Order of St. Benedict. Due to the extinction of the religious orders in 1833/34, the Monastery was utterly forgotten and its assets were sold at public auction. The recovery plan began in 1986 after the building was purchased by the Portuguese State.

4 BRAGA SÉ CATHEDRAL
Dated from the 12th century, was built by the order of Henrique and Teresa, parents of Portugal's first King – Afonso Henriques. Their tombs are to be found inside the Museum of the Cathedral.

5 BISCAÍNHOS MUSEUM
An example of civil Baroque architecture style which illustrates the noble class lifestyle at the time. The exhibition presents a variety of objects from the 17th and 18th centuries.

6 CITY OF GUIMARÃES
Considered the birthplace of the Nation for its first King – D.Afonso Henriques – was born in the city. Guimarães heritage is well-preserved and defines the authenticity of the medieval era.

7 PENEDA DO GERÊS NATIONAL PARK
This protected area conjugates the exuberant vegetation with the wild animals, allowing its visitors to feel part of the Mountain. It offers a wide range of outdoor activities water or land related.

3 PLACES TO EAT

TABERNA BELGA
Portuguese
€

The most loved place to enjoy the Portuguese *Francesinha*. Make sure you arrive early, even after the last size upgrade it's common to have waiting lines, especially on Fridays and Saturdays.

📞 +351 253 042 708

CENTURIUM RESTAURANTE – BRACARA AUGUSTA
Seafood
€ €

Traditional restaurant of regional food and a great looking building with beautiful architectonic details. The codfish is great!

📞 +351 258 839 090

DEGEMA HAMBURGUERIA ARTESANAL
Portuguese
€

If you're searching for a great hamburger, you should try DeGema. The hamburgers' names are funny and represent popular Portuguese expressions. Ask the waitstaff to explain them to you, it will be amusing.

📞 +351 253 687 262

BLB - BIFANARIA
Tasca

Bifana is one of the most known snacks, along with codfish cake. BLB stands for Braga Loves Bifana, so you'll get some of the finest of the region. *Bifana* is a pork steak sandwich made out of rustic bread and specially seasoned meat. Their main menu includes *rojões* (pork), gizzards, tempuras, ham and, of course, *bifana*.

📞 +351 253 138 965

3 PLACES TO SLEEP

MELIA BRAGA HOTEL & SPA
⭐ ⭐ ⭐ ⭐ ⭐
4KM

Great looking hotel near the University. It's very spacious, with delightful common areas and exterior pool. Its restaurant is a hit or miss.

📞 +351 253 144 000
✉️ melia.braga@meliaportugal.com

MERCURE BRAGA CENTRO
⭐ ⭐ ⭐ ⭐
1KM

Standard hotel placed right in the middle of the main city avenue. Very comfortable and with a friendly environment.

📞 +351 253 206 000
✉️ h8308@accor.com

HOTEL DO PARQUE
⭐ ⭐ ⭐ ⭐
6KM

If you like to be around natural environments, you'll love Hotel do Parque. It's right on top of the Natural Park of Bom Jesus, which provides a peaceful and relaxed atmosphere.

✉️ reservas@hoteldoparque.com

⚠️ AREAS TO AVOID

- Bairro de Santa Tecla
- Bairro das Enguardas
- Picoto

BUCKET LIST

- [ ] Taste a *Frigideira* at Frigideiras do Cantinho (pie)
- [ ] Cross the Arch of Rua do Souto, the gateway to the city center
- [ ] Watch a show/concert or visit an exhibition at GNRation space
- [ ] Find the two roosters at Igreja de Santa Cruz façade
- [ ] Eat *Pão com Chouriço* (meat delicacy)
- [ ] Climb Bom Jesus do Monte walking or in cable car
- [ ] Have a picnic at Bom Jesus
- [ ] Row a boat at Bom Jesus
- [ ] Take a panoramic picture of the astonishing view of Sameiro Sanctuary
- [ ] Watch a *Rancho* performance/show (typical music)
- [ ] Taste *Caldo Verde* (soup)
- [ ] Take a walking tour at Peneda do Gerês National Park
- [ ] Take a picture at Portugal's birthplace in Guimarães city center
- [ ] Put a padlock in Toural square at Guimarães
- [ ] Visit the country's biggest Fair in Barcelos (every Thursday)

SPECIAL DATES

- Holy Week Festivals – Easter season
- Braga Romana (May)
- St. João Festival (June 24th – Municipal Holiday)
- White Night (September)

SHOPPING

- Shopping Braga Parque – Avenida Antero de Quental
- Bragashopping – Avenida Central, 33
- Nova Arcada Shopping – Avenida de 100
- Minho Center – Avenida Robert Smith
- Rua do Souto

HOW TO GET TO

🚗 CAR
Porto: 🕐1h00 🛣️A3
Lisboa: 🕐4h00 🛣️A1, A3

🚆 TRAIN
Porto: 🕐1h00 🚆U ➡️ Braga
Lisboa: 🕐3h30 🚆AP ➡️ Braga

🚌 BUS
Porto: 🕐1h15
Lisboa: 🕐5h00

ℹ️ CITY TRANSPORTATION
Bus: TUB – www.tub.pt/

PRICE RATING

VILA REAL

Located on a plateau, bathed by river Corgo and surrounded by mountains, Vila Real (Royal Village) it was once known as the North Court. The innumerous old buildings with the original coats of arms and stunning stone façades stimulate the curiosity among its visitors.

DID YOU KNOW THAT...

Vila Real is the birthplace of Diogo Cão, a famous navigator of the 15th century. Diogo Cão was the first navigator to reach the Cape of Good Hope – peninsula outside Cape Town, South Africa.

He was also the first navigator using stone marks confirming his presence at a determined location.

7 PLACES TO VISIT

1 VILA REAL SÉ CATHEDRAL
Late gothic architecture from the 15th century. A particular note to the cathedral's modern symphonic organ and the altar's gilded carvings.

2 HOUSE OF DIOGO CÃO
Birthplace of the 15th century Portuguese navigator Diogo Cão. Recognized for the epoch architecture, it comprehends round arches and a small curved structure that connects the house to the adjacent building.

3 VILA VELHA MUSEUM
Opened to the public in 2008 it unveils the history of the city of Vila Real, integrating a collection of a hundred objects from the Bronze Age until the contemporary era.

4 S. PAULO'S CHURCH/NEW CHAPEL
Situated in the historical center, this elegant temple is a baroque construction from the 18th century. Characterized by its imponent façade, the Church remodeling was attributed to the renowned Italian architect Nicolao Nazoni.

5 PANÓIAS SANCTUARY
Built in the transition from the 2nd to the 3rd century, the temples were dedicated to the infernal deities. In the place were held initiation rituals, culminating with death, burial and symbolic resurrection of the novices.

6 MATEUS PALACE
Dated from the 18th century, the Palace accommodates a library with around 6.000 specimens, including an illustrated copy of one of the most famous literary Portuguese works – *Os Lusíadas*.

7 FISGAS DO ERMELO WATERFALL (MONDIM DE BASTO)
One of the largest waterfalls in Europe with 200 meters long. At the source of the waterfall, there's a cluster of crystal water lagoons recurrently used by the sunbathers in the Summer season.

3 PLACES TO EAT **3 PLACES TO SLEEP**

CAIS DA VILLA

Meat
€ € €

Excellent restaurant with a beautiful modern look located next to the train station. It offers a wide range of fine wines from the Douro region. Local meats are highly recommended.
+351 259 351 209

CASA DE PASTO CHAXOILA

Mediterranean
€ €

Right outside Vila Real, this restaurant celebrates more than 70 years of service, providing some of the best Trás-os-Montes region tidbits. Their main treats are the typical codfish tempuras, smoked ham and *tripas aos molhos* – pork tripe. It was recently remodeled, but it didn't lose its regional cuisine roots.
+351 259 322 654

CASTAS E PRATOS

Meat
€ € €

If you can add 30km to your trip, we recommend you this restaurant at Peso da Régua situated at an old train warehouse. A tremendous wining and dining experience.
+351 254 323 290

TRALHA WINE TAPAS BAR

Tasca

A pleasing place to have some tapas with a group of friends. For those who need a nap after the meal, the Carreira's garden is right on the other side of the street.
+351 253 206 260

HOTEL MIRACORGO

⭐⭐⭐⭐
1KM

The Hotel Mira Corgo is located in the historical center. It provides a nice view of the surrounding nature. Although the exterior looks a bit old-fashioned, the quality and comfort definitely are there.
+351 259 325 001
reservas@hotelmiracorgo.com

BORRALHA GUEST HOUSE

Guesthouse
2KM

Placed in a recovered old mansion, this guest house offers hospitality and a viable option to enjoy the calmness of the city. It's not easy to find and the access is made via a narrow street.
+351 259 375 158
reservations@borralhaguesthouse.com

HOTEL QUINTA DO PAÇO

⭐⭐⭐⭐
5KM

Constructed on top of an 18th century farmhouse, this hotel shows a lot of character through its granary, ponds, fountains and reading corners. It could use some renewed room decoration.
259 340 790
hotel@quintapaco.com

BUCKET LIST ✓

- ☐ Taste *Cristas de Galo* (pastry)
- ☐ Climb to São Leonardo de Galafura viewpoint and watch the sunset
- ☐ Take the Corgo Park pedestrian trail
- ☐ Have a picnic at Alvão Natural Park
- ☐ Eat *Covilhetes* (pie)
- ☐ Bathe in a lagoon at Alvão Natural Park
- ☐ Buy a Bisalhão handicraft
- ☐ Taste *Pito de Santa Luzia* (pastry)
- ☐ Visit University of Trás-os-Montes Botanical Garden
- ☐ Taste a *Gancha* (candy)
- ☐ Taste *Cavacórios* (pastry)
- ☐ Cross the Red Bridge
- ☐ Drink a *Traçadinho* (alcoholic drink)
- ☐ See a play at Vila Real Municipal Theater
- ☐ Ride a kart at Kartódromo Vila Real

SPECIAL DATES ☆

- St. António Festival (June 13th – Municipal Holiday)
- Rock Nordeste Summer Festival (June)
- WTCC – FIA World Touring Car Championship (June)
- FAG – Handicrafts and Gastronomy Fair (November)

SHOPPING

- Nosso Shopping – Alameda de Grasse

PRICE RATING

HOW TO GET TO

🚗 CAR
Porto: 🕐1h00 🛣A4
Lisboa: 🕐4h00 🛣A1, A4

🚆 TRAIN
Porto: 🕐2h00 🚆IR ➡ Régua
Lisboa: 🕐5h00 🚆AP ➡ Porto – Campanhã
⇄ IR ➡ Régua

To get to Vila Real city center in 30 minutes take the city transportation (Auto Viação do Tâmega).

🚌 BUS
Porto: 🕐2h00
Lisboa: 🕐5h00

ℹ CITY TRANSPORTATION
Bus: Autoviação do Tâmega – <u>www. avtamega.pt</u>

PORTO

In the mouth of the Douro river, Porto breathes life. The old and charming *Invicta* (unvanquished city) full of history, architecture and culture is part of the UNESCO World Heritage. Considered the Best European Destination 3 times in the past decade, it is impossible to resist its glamour and attractiveness. Porto offers you a host of liveliness markets, enchanting restaurants, and superb viewpoints.

DID YOU KNOW THAT...

Manoel de Oliveira, born and raised in Porto, was the eldest active cinematographer in the world. His last movie *O Velho do Restelo* was released a month after completing 106 years old. The famous cinematographer passed away in 2015 at the same age.

10 PLACES TO VISIT

1 CASA DA MÚSICA
A magnificent cultural venue designed by the Dutch architect Rem Koolhaas. The Casa da Música (House of Music) hosts major international productions or small-scale experimental projects.

2 SERRALVES PARK
Right in the very heart of Porto, Serralves Park offers an array of exciting elements, like well-tended gardens, woods, a Romantic lake and the Serralves Museum of Contemporary Art. The perfect spot to escape from the bustle of the city.

3 LELLO BOOKSHOP
Claimed to be one of the best and most beautiful bookshops in the world, its crimson staircases inspired the author of Harry Potter – J.K. Rolling.

4 CLÉRIGOS TOWER
Another Portuguese work of art by the hands of Nicolau Nasoni dated from the 18th century. The top of the tower offers one of the most amazing panoramic views of the city.

5 PORTO WINE CELLARS
A Portuguese ex-libris that document an unusual history of temperance and courage. Guided tours available for deepening knowledge about the Port wine and the Douro region through a wine tasting experience.

6 RIBEIRA
One of the most ancient and typical sites in Porto, where the smell of the sardines breaches the air, and the strong accent is genuine.

7 PALÁCIO DA BOLSA (STOCK EXCHANGE)
A beautiful 19thcentury neoclassical building designed by the Porto architect Joaquim da Costa Lima Júnior. Its centerpieces include the main courtyard named Hall of Nations and the Arab Hall, where the most important official ceremonies in the city were once held.

8 CRYSTAL PALACE GARDENS
This scenic and pleasant park, located in the city center, provides superb panoramic views over the Douro river and the sea. The Crystal Palace, surrounded by a variety of plants and birds' species, serves as a venue for concerts and sports events.

9 PORTO SÉ CATHEDRAL
Romanesque construction from the 12th century that still exhibits a fortress-like figure. A special mention goes to the gilded carvings and the tiles in the cloister.

10 FOZ (RIVER MOUTH)
Known as the most expensive zone in the city, *Foz* invites you to go for a stroll by the sea. This recreational and healthy area is a magnet for the photography lovers.

7 PLACES TO EAT

ANTIQVVM
Mediterranean
€ € €

This restaurant has it all: great location by the Douro river, great food, and of course, great wines. There are no visual clues of it from the outside, pay extra attention when searching for this restaurant.
📞 +351 226 000 445

O PAPARICO
Mediterranean
€ € €

Another fantastic restaurant placed just outside the city center. This is one of those places you'll remember, a parallel dimension as they say. Unforgettable tasting menu.
📞 +351 225 400 548

WINE QUAY BAR
Meat
€ €

This bar offers an extensive selection of Tapas and wines to enjoy with a marvelous view over the Douro river.

Being a bar, you'll sense the casual environment and good vibes. Ask for the outside seats if the weather permits.
📞 +351 222 080 119

THE YEATMAN RESTAURANT
Mediterranean
€ € €

As expected from a 2 Michelin-stars restaurant, the Yeatman gourmet dishes will be a delight for the eyes and the taste buds. Chef Ricardo Costa offers imaginative cuisine and blends traditional Portuguese flavors with contemporary flair. Placed on the top floor of the Yeatman hotel, this restaurant provides excellent service and ambiance, with a breathtaking panoramic view over the Douro River.
📞 +351 220 133 100

TAPABENTO
Seafood
€ €

Tapabento Restaurant & Bar is located in downtown Porto, near S. Bento Railway Station, in an old traditional building.
It's an appealing option for a lighter meal, specialized in seafood tapas: mussels, clams, oysters, shrimps, and carpaccios. A wide selection of wines will certainly help you enjoy these treats.
📞 +351 912 881 272

ESCONDIDINHO DO BARREDO
Tasca

The *tasca* name, also known as Tasca da Cremilda says it all – Little Hidden Place of Barredo.

Placed at a narrow street and missing external signs (search for the red door with views for the kitchen area), this old *tasca* offers Porto's most famous tidbits: *Iscas de Bacalhau* – battered and deep-fried codfish fillets.

You can also try the octopus, stuffed potato balls or fried cuttlefish.

📞 +351 222 057 229

BAR SOARES

Tasca

If you cross the Douro river to the south and walk by the Gaia bay, we suggest you the fried codfish cakes at Bar Soares. It's next to a multitude of restaurants, but its simplicity, and traditional roots will offer an appealing feel of the Portuguese fisherman families. You'll find an offer of sea products, most of them served grilled.

📞 +351 910 868 480

5 PLACES TO SLEEP
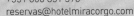

INTERCONTINENTAL PORTO – CARDOSAS PALACE

⭐⭐⭐⭐
Center

This beautiful hotel lies right at the end of the city main avenue – Avenida dos Aliados. Born from a renovated 18th century palace, the hotel is the ideal place for those looking to experience the city's charm.

📞 +351 800 831 390

✉ reservas@hotelmiracorgo.com

THE YEATMAN HOTEL

⭐⭐⭐⭐⭐
5KM

Yeatman is a luxurious hotel on one of Gaia's slopes, facing the Douro river and the Ribeira.

Set amidst the Port wine lodges, it offers indoor and outdoor infinity pools, an award-winning restaurant, a fantastic Caudalie SPA and 82 rooms themed with wine brands. It's the tourists favorite choice to stay in Porto if you don't mind the extra distance to the center.

📞 +351 220 133 18

✉ reservations@theyeatman.com

TOREL AVANTGARDE

⭐⭐⭐⭐⭐
1KM

This recently made five-star boutique hotel provides a fresh take on decoration themes and art placement. The innovation can be interpreted all through the hall suspended flowers, by the 47 distinct rooms with beautiful paintings and composition and the wine walls at Digby's restaurant.

A culturally rich experience with a panoramic view over the Douro river environment.

📞 +351 220 110 082

✉ info@torelavantgarde.com

THE ARTIST PORTO HOTEL & BISTRO

⭐⭐⭐⭐
1KM

A trendy looking Hotel with a comfortable and contemporary ambiance, which used to be a hat factory. It also serves as the school-hotel for the students of the Porto School of Tourism.

📞 +351 220 132 700

✉ geral@theartistporto.pt

INPATIO GUEST HOUSE

Guesthouse
Center

InPatio is located in a restored late 19th century building in the Ribeira quarter, managed by a caring couple. The bedrooms aren't large, but the stylish and distinct decoration definitely compensates it.

📞 +351 222 085 477

✉ reservations@borralhaguesthouse.com

SPECIAL DATES

- Fantasporto – Porto International Film Festival (February)
- Serralves Festival (June)
- St. João Festival (June 24th – Municipal Holiday)
- Meo Marés Vivas Summer Festival (July) – Matosinhos
- Noites Ritual Summer Festival (September)
- Comic Con Portugal (December) – Leça da Palmeira

HOW TO GET TO

🚗 CAR
Lisboa: 🕐3h00 🛣A1

🚆 TRAIN
Lisboa: 🕐2h45 🚉AP ➡ Porto

🚇 METRO
Aeroporto station: 🕐0h30 🚉 Purple line (E) ➡ Trindade station

🚌 BUS
Lisboa: 🕐3h30min

ℹ CITY TRANSPORTATION
Bus: Sociedade de Transportes Colectivos do Porto (STCP) – www.stcp.pt
Metro: Metro do Porto – www.metrodoporto.pt

SHOPPING

- NorteShopping – Rua Sara Afonso, Senhora da Hora (Matosinhos)
- ViaCatarina Shopping – Rua de Santa Catarina
- Alameda Shop&Spot – Rua dos Campeões Europeus
- Rua de Santa Catarina
- Rua de Cedofeita
- Rua das Carmelitas
- Rua dos Clérigos

AREAS TO AVOID ⚠

- Bairro do Aleixo
- Bairro do Cerco
- Bairro do Lagarteiro
- Bairro da Pasteleira
- Bairro Pinheiro Torres

PRICE RATING €

€ € € € €

BUCKET LIST

- [ ] Eat a *Francesinha* (regional delicacy)
- [ ] Take a picture at Avenida dos Aliados
- [ ] Drink a coffee/tea at the historic Majestic Café
- [ ] Take the Funicular (cable car) to or from Batalha
- [ ] Take a picture at D. Luís I Bridge
- [ ] Listen to *Fado* in front of the Douro river
- [ ] Eat grilled sardines in Ribeira
- [ ] Embrace the adventure at the World of Discoveries Museum
- [ ] Watch the sunset at Jardim do Morro (Vila Nova de Gaia)
- [ ] Cruise along the Douro river
- [ ] Check out the view from the Monastery of Serra do Pilar
- [ ] Pay a visit to Mercado do Bolhão
- [ ] Try *Tripas à Moda do Porto* (tripe)
- [ ] Buy a tile as a souvenir
- [ ] Eat *Bacalhau à Gomes de Sá* (codfish)
- [ ] Have a meal at Mercado do Bom Sucesso
- [ ] Go for a taste of contemporary art and design at Rua Miguel Bombarda
- [ ] Check out the collection of trophies from the F.C.Porto football team at Estádio do Dragão Museum.
- [ ] Get to know the transports used by our ancestries at the Tram Museum.
- [ ] Try a nautical sport at Matosinhos beach

BRAGANÇA

Looking for the most delicious smoked food and jams in the World? Welcome to Bragança! This picturesque city embraced by nature and full of Roman-influenced constructions it also gave its name to the last of the Portuguese royal lineage, the House of Bragança. Its small and rural environment introduces you to the friendliest people in Portugal.

DID YOU KNOW THAT...

The Celts inhabited the North of Portugal for many centuries leaving behind some of its cultural traditions – *Caretos* are one of its best representations. Its colorful, noisy, mysterious and diabolic figures are known to scare people and disturbing the daily calm during Carnival.

7 PLACES TO VISIT

1 CASTLE OF BRAGANÇA
Located in the heart of the old city, this well-preserved architecture work of art had once an important defense role in Bragança. The Military Museum inside the Tower revives the memory of the military experience of its villagers.

2 CHURCH OF SANTA MARIA
The oldest church in Bragança dates from the 17th century and follows the baroque style. The scenography painting to be founded in its interior represents the Assumption of the Virgin Mary.

3 IBERIAN MUSEUM OF MASK AND COSTUME
Museum dedicated to the promotion of the Mask and the Costume traditions of the northeastern region and the city of Zamora (Spain).

4 DOMUS MUNICIPALIS
Unique and still enigmatic monument of Romanesque civil architecture. Generally thought to have been used as a cistern for suppressing the local population needs of water, during times of drought.

5 CASTRO DE AVELÃS MONASTERY
The remains of this Romanesque church, are known as the chosen location for the Duke of Lancaster to stay overnight prior to meeting with King João I for the signing of the treaty of Babe (March 26th 1387). The signature earned the Duke the hand of the Kings' daughter, Filipa of Lancaster, in marriage.

6 RIO DE ONOR TRADITIONAL VILLAGE
A communitarian village filled with old schist houses and porched balconies. The river beach, the windmills, and the ancient monuments are part of the landscape.

7 MAZOUCO ROCK ART (FREIXO DE ESPADA À CINTA)
First outdoor Paleolithic rock art station discovered in Portugal (1981). The figure was engraved on a schist surface by perforation and abrasion techniques.

3 PLACES TO EAT

3 PLACES TO SLEEP

RESTAURANTE SOLAR BRAGANÇANO

€

Meat

With a modest looking façade, the interior feels like an old noble mansion. A place to taste the traditional meat dishes of Trás-os-Montes. You should try the *Alheira* and *Posta à Mirandesa*.

📞 +351 273 323 875

POUSADA DE BRAGANCA

Mediterranean

€ € €

Offers modern cuisine with a fancy view over Bragança Castle. A nice place to try local food with a unique experience.

📞 +351 273 331 493

CASA NOSTRA

Italian

€

A modest looking restaurant with delicious Pizzas. If you want to have something lighter after trying Brangança's famous meat, this is a nice alternative.

📞 +351 273 382 221

TASCA DO ZÉ TUGA

Tasca

Right by the Brangança Castle, this *tasca* offers "tapas, wine, and conversation". We recommend the *costelas mendinhas de porco* (pork chops) and *alheira*. While the ambiance really feels like a *tasca*, its owner, and chef Luís Portugal creates traditional dishes with some positive and innovative twists.

📞 +351 273 381 358

POUSADA DE BRAGANÇA - SAO BARTOLOMEU

Inn

1KM

Located aside the Fervença river, it provides magnificent views of the city's medieval castle. The rooms are big and each one has a private balcony to enjoy the beautiful rural setting. You can easily get to the city by walking for 15 minutes.

📞 +351 273 331 493

✉ reservas@hotelmiracorgo.com

HOTEL SANTA APOLONIA

⭐ ⭐ ⭐

2KM

A simpler alternative that offers good service for a fair price. The room beds look a bit old-fashioned, but the overall feeling is favorable. The breakfast includes some local treats.

📞 +351 273 313 219

✉ santa_apolonia@iol.pt

QUINTA DA RICA-FÉ.

Farmhouse

3KM

Being a 300 years old farmhouse, you can follow its history in every decorative element, resembling a museum. Each of the five rooms is unique, and the family that runs it provide a very helpful service.

📞 +351 967 574 179

PRICE RATING

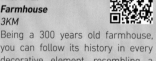

€ € € € €

BUCKET LIST ✅

- [ ] Wander the citadel streets and cover the entire extension of the Wall walking
- [ ] Take a panoramic photo from the top of the Torre de Menagem
- [ ] Eat a *Posta* (meat dish)
- [ ] Watch a *Pauliteiros de Miranda* Show
- [ ] See or play a match of *Jogo do Fito* (traditional game)
- [ ] Try Braganças' famous chestnuts, jams, and rosemary honey
- [ ] Walk down the Museum Street and visit the exhibitions (Rua Abílio Beça)
- [ ] Check out the view from the Shrine of St. Bartolomeu viewpoint
- [ ] Take the Vilarinho pedestrian trail at Montesinho Natural Park
- [ ] Have a picnic at Azibo's dam
- [ ] Visit the artisanal Razors' shop in Aveleda village
- [ ] Check out the picturesque houses made of schist in the quiet and genuine Rio de Onor village
- [ ] Cross the border to Spain in Rio de Onor village
- [ ] Try the traditional smoked foods in one of Gimonde's restaurants
- [ ] Cross the Onor river using the stepping stone between the Roman bridge and the granitic bridge (Gimonde)

SPECIAL DATES ⭐

- Butelo and Casulas Festival (February)
- Cantarinhas Market (2nd and 3rd of May)
- Handicraft Fair (May)
- Festa da História (Medieval Fair, middle August)
- Nossa Senhora das Graças Festival (August 22nd – Municipal Holiday)

SHOPPING 🛍

- Bragança Shopping – Avenida Sá Carneiro, nº 2
- Rua Almirante Reis

HOW TO GET TO 🧭

🚗 CAR
Porto: 🕒2h30 🛣A4
Lisboa: 🕒5h00 🛣A1, A25, A24, IP4

🚆 TRAIN
Unavailable

🚌 BUS
Porto: 🕒3h00
Lisboa: 🕒7h00

ℹ CITY TRANSPORTATION
Bus: STUB – www.cm-braganca.pt/pages/114

CENTER

Leiria

North Atlantic Ocean

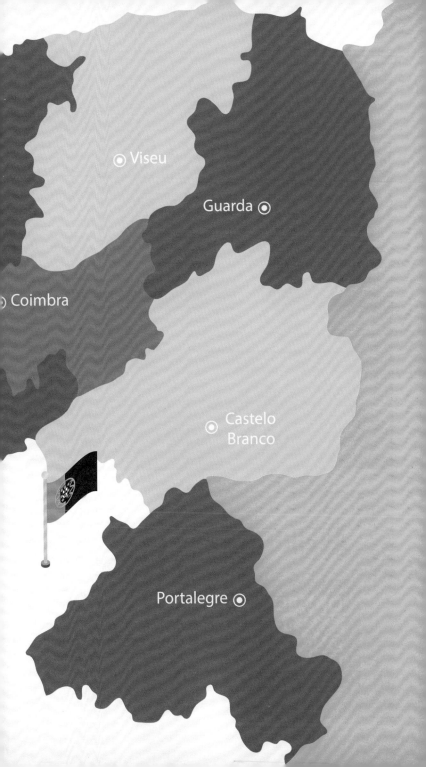

AVEIRO

The water channels and colorful vessels of this charismatic city are a genuine representation of the harmony between land and sea. The natural water landscape, together with its romanticism and salty history, converted Aveiro into the Portuguese Venice. Surrender yourself to the city's uniquely sweet flavors and vibrant creativity.

DID YOU KNOW THAT...

Ovos Moles were the first Portuguese pastry to be distinguished by the European Commission as PGI – Protected Geographical Indication. This certification assures the quality of the dessert and the traditional preparation method (following the original recipe entirely), perpetuating and preserving the ancient knowledge transmitted across generations.

7 PLACES TO VISIT

1 RIA DE AVEIRO
The habitat for an enormous ecological wealth, keeping alive a variety of fish species, seaweed, and birds. Its characteristic appearance is paved with endless intersections and islands.

2 FISH SQUARE
Dated from the first decade of the 20th century, the Fish Square is one of the most distinctive and privileged locations of the city. This particular example of iron architecture daily witnesses the rushed Aveiro nightlife.

3 AVEIRO MUSEUM
Located inside the Monastery of Jesus, the museum exhibits paintings, sculptures, gold carvings, tiles, jewelry and textiles from the 14th and 15th centuries.

4 AVEIRO SÉ CATHEDRAL
Known as a former part of a Dominican convent from the 15th century, it was the first religious community to be established in the city. The three Human Virtues (Faith, Hope, and Charity) are represented in its façade along with the coat of arms of Infante D. Pedro (the King's son).

5 COSTA NOVA HOUSES
Traditional structures used by fishermen as storage and shelters throughout the 19th century. Nowadays, the houses, painted in bright-colored stripes, became a massive tourist attraction as beach residences.

6 BARRA BEACH LIGHTHOUSE
The tallest lighthouse in Portugal and one of the tallest in Europe (60 meters above sea level), marks the spot where the Ria de Aveiro meets the sea. 271 stone steps of adventure through a spiral staircase that leads to the top of the lighthouse.

7 NATURE RESERVE DUNAS DE ST. JACINTO
This supremely peaceful protected area consists of an extensive line of sand dunes, bordered by a forested hillside. Different tree species were planted in the late 19th century to bring stability to the sands.

3 PLACES TO EAT

SALPOENTE
 Mediterranean
€ € €

Located by the São Roque canal, this modern building was once a salt warehouse. The Mediterranean menu is diverse, but it's well known for the salt codfish.

☎ +351 234 382 674

A PEIXARIA
Seafood
€ €

A simple looking restaurant that directs to the humble fisherman neighborhood, so don't expect great decor. It makes a perfect trip across Torreira since you have to get to the tip of the peninsula (you can get by ferryboat). They excel in the fish preparation, which gives it the name "The Fish Market."

☎ +351 234 331 165

O BATISTA DO BACALHAU
Seafood
€

Another expert restaurant in codfish recipes. It has a large choice of wines and a generous main area. We suggest the grilled codfish with squashed potatoes.

☎ +351 234 341 949

TASCA DO SAL
Tasca

This rustic tasca, right by the ria, offers some of the best tidbits in Aveiro. We suggest starting with the ham and cheese and quickly scale to the squid, octopus and scrambled eggs with sausage.

If the weather is warm, enjoy the terrace.

☎ +351 234 096 267

3 PLACES TO SLEEP

HOTEL MOLICEIRO
★ ★ ★ ★
4KM

A sophisticated hotel by the ria; it has 15 thematic rooms to choose from like Chanel, Oriental or Romantic. Very sympathetic and refined service. They provide live music near the bar on Fridays and Saturdays.

☎ +351 234 337 400
✉ melia.braga@meliaportugal.com

MELIA RIA HOTEL & SPA
★ ★ ★ ★
Center

Its innovative shape resembles a huge ice cube falling into the river. It offers a nice panoramic view of the ria with a modern design and equipment.

☎ +351 234 401 000
✉ melia.ria@meliaportugal.com

OC SALON CHARM HOSTEL & SUITES
Guesthouse
Center

Set in a completely rebuilt 19th century building, OC Salon's rooms are decorated with charming modern furniture. It has a private bathroom option.
It is within walking range from a grand variety of restaurants and landmarks.

☎ +351 234 067 063

⚠ AREAS TO AVOID

• Bairro de Santiago

BUCKET LIST

- [ ] Get to know the city in a Moliceiro (boat)
- [ ] Taste Pão-de-Ló from Ovar (pastry)
- [ ] Find your zodiac sign in the pavement of Marquês de Pombal Square
- [ ] Taste Ovos Moles (pastry)
- [ ] Take the Paiva walkways tour (Arouca)
- [ ] Travel around the city by BUGA (city free bicycles)
- [ ] Cross the lagoon to St. Jacinto in a ferry-boat
- [ ] Try Águeda pastries
- [ ] Walk on the Barra Beach sand
- [ ] Take the Vouguinha to Águeda city – Portugal's oldest train
- [ ] Taste Tripas de Aveiro (pastry)
- [ ] Take a walk at the City Park – Infante D. Pedro Park
- [ ] Observe the seabirds at the Nature Reserve Dunas de St. Jacinto
- [ ] Check out the Ílhavo Maritime Museum (Ílhavo)
- [ ] Take a picture at the "I <3 Aveiro" staircase

SPECIAL DATES

- St. Gonçalinho Festival (January)
- Feira de Março (March – April)
- St. Joana, the Princess Festival (May 12th – Municipal Holiday)
- Ílhavo Codfish Festival (August)

SHOPPING

- Forum Aveiro – Rua do Batalhão de Caçadores, 10
- Centro Comercial Glicínias Plaza – Rua Dom Manuel Barbuda e Vasconcelos
- Aveiro Shopping Center – Estrada da Taboeira
- Avenida Lourenço Peixinho

HOW TO GET TO

🚗 CAR
Porto: 🕐 0h50 🛣️ A1
Lisboa: 🕐 2h30 🛣️ A1

🚆 TRAIN
Porto: 🕐 0h30 🚆 AP ➡️ Aveiro
Lisboa: 🕐 2h15 🚆 AP ➡️ Aveiro

🚌 BUS
Porto: 🕐 2h00
Lisboa: 🕐 3h30

ℹ️ CITY TRANSPORTATION
Bus: Aveiro Bus – www.aveirobus.pt

PRICE RATING

VISEU

Crossed by crystal-clear rivers and nestled in the mountains, Viseu was elected as the best city to live in Portugal. The rugged landscapes and thermal waters are home to renowned wine producers and artisans.

Enjoy the hospitality of its people and the affordable cost of living.

DID YOU KNOW THAT...

The city hero is a warrior named Viriato. He was the Lusitanian Chief between 147 and 139 BC and defeated several Roman armies. The archetypal hero halted the advance of invaders and demonstrated exceptional leadership qualities. A city fortification was named after him – Cava de Viriato. This relationship to Viseu has been immortalized in the Statue of Viriato, which stands beside the Cava.

7 PLACES TO VISIT

1 VISEU SÉ CATHEDRAL
Its massive and austere appearance make the exterior of the Cathedral impressive. Nevertheless, the most exciting aspect of the building is its interior, underlining the Manueline ceiling. Stairs in the northern transept of the cathedral lead to the Arte Sacra Museum and to the cloister.

2 MISERICÓRDIA CHURCH
The bright rococo façade of the 18th century contrasts with the severity of the courtyard conferred by the Sé Cathedral. Of particular note is the lovely balcony and the two towers decorated with large windows.

3 ROMAN WALL
A so-called open-air museum built by the Romans from the 1st century on. While wandering the Formosa Street, a glass plate on the ground can be seen, leaving History at the people's feet.

4 CAVA DE VIRIATO
An ancient Roman camp, believed to be built by the Lusitanians, considered an archaeological mystery. The octagon fortress suffered from the erosion of time and was requalified in 2001.

5 GRÃO VASCO NATIONAL MUSEUM
Founded in 1915 it houses a remarkable set of paintings from the local artist, Grão Vasco. The collection of objects and images has been expanded to include some archaeological pieces, porcelain, and furniture.

6 RUA DIREITA
This narrow cobbled street, widely recognized as an important commercial site, presents tremendous archeological value to the Region, with deep Roman influences in its construction.

7 FONTELO PARK
Situated in the historical center, this spacious leisure area brings together both natural and cultural heritage. Besides practicing sports, it is possible to observe essential monuments of the city.

3 PLACES TO EAT

MURALHA DA SÉ

 Mediterranean

€ €

A unique restaurant with a pleasant location directly opposite the Cathedral of Viseu. It has a small entrance hall and a warm dining room with stone walls and a fireplace. The perfect establishment to enjoy traditional Portuguese cuisine right at the heart of the city.

📞 +351 232 437 777

RUI PAULA DOC RESTAURANTE

Mediterranean

€ € €

A fabulous restaurant with a breathtaking view over the Douro river. It's chef, Rui Paula, provides highly innovative dishes and presentation. A must-go if you can take the detour; it's perfect if you're heading north to Vila Real.

📞 +351 254 858 123

CASA AROUQUESA

Steakhouse

€ €

An exquisite restaurant, where special attention is paid to the speed of service and hospitality. If you are a meat lover, you can't leave this region without experiencing the succulent meats on the menu.

📞 +351 234 331 165

TABERNA DA MILINHA

Tasca

With half a dozen tables, this tasca is run by a couple of tidbit lovers. You will be able to try more than 24 snacks, ranging from the tavern classics – cheeses and sausages, cod and octopus fritters, slices of roasted pork meat, gizzards or shrimp with lime.

📞 +351 969 700 056

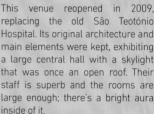 # 3 PLACES TO SLEEP

POUSADA DE VISEU

★ ★ ★ ★

Center

This venue reopened in 2009, replacing the old São Teotónio Hospital. Its original architecture and main elements were kept, exhibiting a large central hall with a skylight that was once an open roof. Their staff is superb and the rooms are large enough; there's a bright aura inside of it.

📞 +351 232 457 320
✉ recepcao.viseu@pousadas.pt

SIX SENSES DOURO VALLEY

★ ★ ★ ★ ★

73KM

Right by the Douro river. It offers luxury tourism at one of the most amazing landscapes of the country. Not only does it provide a great deal of detail in its decoration and common areas, but the surrounding zone deserves to be lived and absorbed.

📞 +351 253 206 000
✉ h8308@accor.com

MONTEBELO VISEU CONGRESS HOTEL

★ ★ ★ ★ ★

6KM

Montebelo Hotel is placed on a small hill at the city center, with a pleasant view of its surroundings.
It has both internal and external swimming pools, a jacuzzi and Turkish bath. The rooms are reasonably sized and quite comfortable.

📞 +351 232 420 000

BUCKET LIST

- [ ] Try Sopa da Beira (soup)
- [ ] Take a picture with the Viriato statue
- [ ] Get to know the city by tourist train
- [ ] Have a picnic at Fontelo Park
- [ ] Take a picture of the Wall of Painted Tiles by Joaquim Lopes
- [ ] Go for wine tasting at Dão Wines Route Welcome Center
- [ ] Take the Ribeira da Várzea pedestrian trail
- [ ] Taste Doces de Ovos de Viseu (pastry)
- [ ] Take a free ride in the Funicular (cable car)
- [ ] Visit the live beach (June to September – Mangualde)
- [ ] Climb to Caramulinho viewpoint (Caramulo) on a sunny day to watch the sea
- [ ] Try cherries from Resende
- [ ] Take a picture with the armored Mercedes at Caramulo Museum
- [ ] Buy a Tibaldinho embroidery as a souvenir
- [ ] Go skating at the ice ring of Palácio de Gelo Shopping mall

SPECIAL DATES

- Cavalhadas de Vildemoinhos (June 24th)
- Feira de São Mateus, handicraft fair (August – September)
- St. Mateus Festival (September 21st – Municipal Holiday)

SHOPPING

- Palácio do Gelo Shopping – Rua do Palácio do Gelo, 3
- Fórum Viseu – Rua Dom José da Cruz Moreira Pinto, 32
- Rua Direita de Viseu

AREAS TO AVOID

- Bairro de Paradinha

HOW TO GET TO

🚗 CAR
Porto: 🕐1h30 🛣️A1, A25
Lisboa: 🕐3h00 🛣️A1, IP3

🚉 TRAIN
Unavailable

🚌 BUS
Porto: 🕐2h
Lisboa: 🕐3h30

ℹ️ CITY TRANSPORTATION
Bus: STUV – www.stuv.weebly.com

PRICE RATING

 € € € € €

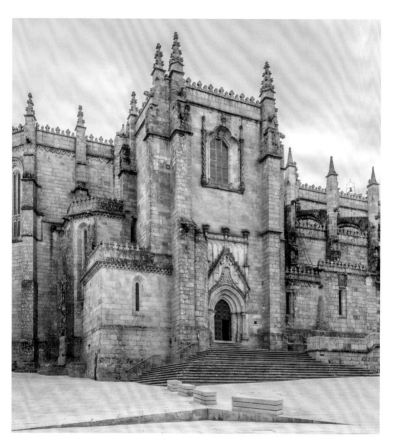

GUARDA

Be overcome by this austere centenary city that once protected the Realm against the Moors and the Spaniards. Feel the bravery of Kings and the strength of battles in its arcaded streets and sober squares. The highest city in Portugal, marked by its imposing buildings, offers endless astonishing views inside and across borders.

DID YOU KNOW THAT...

Guarda is the birthplace of Carolina Beatriz Ângela, the first woman to exercise the right to vote in Portugal, back in 1911. She used the ambiguity of law to her advantage, to cast her vote in the election of the Constituent National Assembly. This issued the right to vote to literate heads-of-household over 21.

7 PLACES TO VISIT

1 THE FORTRESS-LIKE CATHEDRAL
A granite building in fortified shape from the late 14th century. Its construction work was dragged out for over 150 years and mixes the Gothic and Manueline styles.

2 CASTLE OF GUARDA
In a privileged position, it rises to 1000 meters above sea level. Although mostly uncharacterized by continuous interventions, the remaining sections of its old walls still define, in some places, the urban limits.

3 SERRA DA ESTRELA
The second highest mountain in the country is also the most significant protected area on Portuguese soil. Besides the snow and the extraordinary fauna and flora, the human, cultural, historical and gastronomical wealth are top attractions.

4 PORTA DOS FERREIROS, PORTA D'EL REI, AND PORTA DA ERVA
The 12th century city gates mark the entry/exit points of the vast walls of Guarda's defensive system. Only three of the five originals have endured through time.

5 THE ANCIENT JEWISH NEIGHBORHOOD
The Jewish community was once a significant boost for the city of Guarda, leaving some interesting symbols in the streets, as the door crosses.

6 CHURCH OF ST. VICENTE
The baroque façade of this 18th century building is flanked by two bell towers. The historical panels made of tiles located in the church interior are notable to be pointed out.

7 LUÍS DE CAMÕES SQUARE
Noble square in the city center with a different set of porches of Castilian influence, belonging to houses from the 15th to 17th centuries. A great site to spot the Fortress-like Cathedral's north façade.

PLACES TO EAT

 PLACES TO SLEE

DON GARFO
Mediterranean
€ €

This restaurant provides three different romantic modern rooms and two kinds of menus: Sabor and Tradição, that means Taste (modern) and Tradition (classic). Close to the city center, you can quickly get there by foot.

☎ +351 271 211 077

SIMPLE.GUARDA
Italian
€

An inexpensive and relaxed Italian-style restaurant. It's known for the pasta, pizzas and tasty garlic bread.

☎ +351 271 212 149

RESTAURANTE BELO HORIZONTE
Steakhouse
€ €

Located in an old house by the city's historical center this is a traditional restaurant that knows how to use the very best of Guarda's natural resources. Don't forget to try the Queijo da Serra cheese.

☎ +351 271 211 454

A TASQUINHA
Tasca

Very simple and tiny tasca serving fried codfish cakes and rissoles, sardines and traditional vegetable soup. A low-priced and authentic experience by the city center.

☎ +351 271 212 170

HOTEL LUSITÂNIA
★ ★ ★ ★

6KM

Lusitania is a modern hotel just outside the city. The hotel's organic farm is the first of its kind and enables the creation of true healthy menus. The room decor is a bit old-fashioned, but it's compensated for with the courteous service provided and added amenities – two swimming pools, sauna, and jacuzzi.

☎ +351 275 330 406
✉ centraldereservas@ naturaimbhotels.com

CASA DAS PENHAS DOURADAS HOTEL & SPA
★ ★ ★ ★ ★

73KM

If you want to relax and enjoy the mountain scenery, this is where you should rest. Placed in the Natural Park of Serra da Estrela, which was found to have the healthiest air to breath in the country. The design is fantastic with the bonus of a warm family environment and a very professional staff team. An attractive option if you like snow (winter) and if you don't mind getting to such a remote location.

☎ +351 275 981 045
✉ mail@casadaspenhasdouradas.pt

HOTEL VANGUARDA
★ ★ ★

Center

A 10-minute walk from the city center, this simpler and inexpensive hotel offers a wide view of the Guarda's beautiful natural resources.

☎ +351 271 208 390
✉ centraldereservas@ naturaimbhotels.com

BUCKET LIST

- [ ] Eat a Morcela (delicacy)
- [ ] Take a picture with a working shepherd
- [ ] Watch a Capeia Arraiana (bullfight) in August
- [ ] Try a winter sport at Serra da Estrela
- [ ] Take the Galhardos pedestrian trail in Gouveia
- [ ] Check out Marialva historical village
- [ ] Take a picture with King Sancho I statue at Luís de Camões Square
- [ ] Visit the historical village Linhares da Beira (Celorico da Beira)
- [ ] Eat Queijo da Serra (cheese)
- [ ] Watch the almond trees in blossom in February (Figueira de Castelo Rodrigo)
- [ ] Try Arroz Doce (dessert)
- [ ] See the rock art at Vale do Côa Archaeological Park
- [ ] Visit the Praça Forte de Almeida (Almeida)
- [ ] Check out the ancient toys at Museu do Brinquedo (Seia)
- [ ] Bathe in the Waterfall of Poço da Broca (Seia)

SPECIAL DATES

- Guardafolia Carnival parade (February)
- City Festivities (July)
- Feira Farta, local products fair (September)
- Municipal Holiday (November 27th)
- Guarda: City of Christmas (December)

SHOPPING

- LA VIE Guarda Shopping Center – Avenida dos Bombeiros Voluntários Egitanienses
- Rua do Comércio

PRICE RATING

HOW TO GET TO

🚗 CAR
Porto: 🕐2h00 🛣A1; A25
Lisboa: 🕐4h00 🛣A1; A23

🚆 TRAIN
Porto: 🕐3h00 🚆IC ➡ Coimbra-B ⇄ IC ➡ Guarda
Lisboa: 🕐4h15 🚆IC ➡ Guarda

🚌 BUS
Porto: 🕐3h00
Lisboa: 🕐4h30

ℹ CITY TRANSPORTATION
Bus: Transportes Urbanos da Guarda: www.transportes.mun-guarda.pt/

COIMBRA

This poetic, historical, and cultural city it is known as the City of Students, as it is the birthplace of the country's first University. Discover the soul of Portuguese music – Fado – in every person and every corner. Be prepared to feel Saudade – a deep emotional state of nostalgia for the absence of someone or something – as soon as you leave the city. All because Coimbra is feeling.

DID YOU KNOW THAT...

The history of Portugal is marked by a Coimbra royalty love story. Infante (Prince) Pedro had secret romantic meetings with his wife's lady-in-waiting, Inês de Castro. As soon as he widowed, the two decided to live as a married couple, against the King's will. Pedro and Inês lived happily with their three kids for years, nevertheless King Afonso IV, unhappy with the situation and pressured by the court, ordered Inês de Castro to be murdered. History records that in excruciating pain, Pedro led an uprising against his father, hunting and executing Inês' murderers, ripping their hearts out.

7 PLACES TO VISIT

1 SÉ VELHA (OLD CATHEDRAL)
The only Portuguese Romanesque cathedral that survived the Reconquest almost intact. The exterior is reminiscent of a castle, a conventional design among the Cathedrals from that era.

2 JARDIM BOTÂNICO (BOTANIC GARDEN)
Located in the heart of the city, Jardim Botânico was founded in 1772 by the then prime-minister, Marquês de Pombal. The garden covers a total area of over 13 ha, most of which was donated by Benedict monks.

3 MONASTERY OF SANTA CLARA-A-NOVA
The Old Monastery, built in the 12th century became an archeological information center after the turbulent waters of the Mondego river hit it. The Order of St. Claire then moved to the New Monastery, under the instructions of the Queen St. Isabel, whose body rests in a tomb of silver and crystal.

4 MONASTERY OF SANTA CRUZ DE COIMBRA
Dated from the early 11th century, the now National Pantheon houses the mortal remains of Portugal's first king, D. Afonso Henriques and of his firstborn son, Sancho I.

5 ROMAN RUINS AND MUSEUM OF CONÍMBRIGA
The village of the Cooper Age was established as an important center during the Roman Empire until the 9th century. It is one of the widest-known archaeological sites in Portugal.

6 PORTUGAL DOS PEQUENITOS PARK
A Recreational, pedagogical tourist park that represents, in detail and on a reduced scale, a wide range of elements of the Architecture and History of Portugal.

7 PIÓDÃO HISTORICAL VILLAGE
Situated on the slope of the Açor Mountain, Piódão is considered one of the most beautiful villages in the country. It's characterized by schist and slate typical houses and pure natural environment.

3 PLACES TO EAT

ARCADAS RESTAURANTE
Mediterranean
€ € €

This elegant restaurant is part of the Quinta das Lágrimas Hotel in the south part of the Mondego river. It has two classically styled rooms that were once horse stables. Modern cuisine with some traditional touches, providing very appealing *à la carte* menus.

📞 +351 239 802 380

SETE RESTAURANTE
Mediterranean
€ €

Placed right by the Church of Santa Cruz, this modern restaurant takes a fresh look into the Portuguese and Mediterranean cuisine. The menus revolve around the number seven – sete, offering the same number of combinations for starters, menus (meat and vegetarian), wine harmonization and desserts.

📞 +351 239 060 065

CASAS DO BRAGAL
Mediterranean
€ €

Even if it's a bit off course and hard to find, we couldn't forget about Casas do Bragal. It's a cozy restaurant with pleasant atmosphere that includes a rich offer of starters and a well-cooked main menu with the best of the Portuguese cuisine.

📞 +351 271 211 454

ZÉ MANEL DOS OSSOS
Tasca

One of the most known and typical tascas of Coimbra. It's tiny, the decoration is super eccentric and, let's say it, ugly. But the food is as Portuguese as it can get. Make sure you arrive before it opens, (12h30min) otherwise you might wait for 1 to 2 hours.

📞 +351 239 823 790

3 PLACES TO SLEEP

VILA GALÉ COIMBRA
★ ★ ★ ★
2KM

With a magnificent view over the Mondego river and its beautiful external swimming pool, this hotel features a dancing decor theme with plenty of artistic representations of music. The 20 minute walk from the center provides a nice feel of the city.

📞 +351 239 240 000
✉ coimbra.reservas@vilagale.com

CASA DE SÃO BENTO
GuestHouse
Center

Placed right in the center, near the university and the river, this is not your usual hotel. It's a modernized house that looks very trendy with cleverly placed decorations. If you choose the standard room, space won't be abundant, but the design is clean and friendly.

📞 +351 916 220 636
✉ geral@casadesaobento.com

HOTEL QUINTA DAS LÁGRIMAS
★ ★ ★ ★ ★
2KM

A luxury hotel that offers three distinct room themes: palace, garden, and Spa. It features exquisite interior design and a passionate botanical garden, extolling the romanticism of far past.

📞 +351 239 802 380
✉ reservas@quintadaslagrimas.pt

BUCKET LIST

- [ ] Find Inês de Castro's blood mark at Quinta das Lágrimas (Santa Clara village)
- [ ] Try leitão (piglet) at Mealhada
- [ ] Find out the date of the oldest Bible in Biblioteca Joanina (University of Coimbra)
- [ ] Go to a Fado Night at Fado ao Centro
- [ ] Eat a Pastel de Tentúgal (pastry)
- [ ] Take the Militar pedestrian trail at Mata do Buçaco
- [ ] Breath the poetry at Penedo da Saudade
- [ ] Watch a show/concert at Salão Brazil
- [ ] Have a coffee at Café Santa Cruz
- [ ] Delight yourself with Portuguese live music at Diligência Bar
- [ ] Go on a Basófias boat trip along the Mondego river
- [ ] Enjoy the sunset at Serra da Boa Viagem
- [ ] Eat Pastéis de Santa Clara (pastry)
- [ ] Try a nautical sport at Figueira da Foz beach
- [ ] Take a walk/go jogging at Mata Nacional do Choupal

SPECIAL DATES

- Medieval Fair (June)
- Popular Fair (June)
- St. Isabel Festival, even years (July 4th – Municipal Holiday)
- Arts Festival (July)
- Feira das Cebolas – Onions' Fair (August)

AREAS TO AVOID

- Bairro do Ingote
- Bairro da Rosa
- Monte Formoso

PRICE RATING

HOW TO GET TO

🚗 CAR
Porto: ⏱1h20 🛣A1
Lisboa: ⏱2h00 🛣A1

🚆 TRAIN
Porto: ⏱1h05 🚆AP ➡ Coimbra
Lisboa: ⏱1h40 🚆AP ➡ Coimbra

🚌 BUS
Porto: ⏱1h15
Lisboa: ⏱5h00

ℹ CITY TRANSPORTATION
Bus: TUB – www.tub.pt

SHOPPING

- Fórum Coimbra – Avenida José Bonifácio de Andrade e Silva, 1
- Alma Shopping – Rua General Humberto Delgado, 207-211
- Praça 8 de Maio
- Rua Ferreira Borges
- Rua Visconde da Luz

Castelo Branco will transport you to a true twilight zone full of Castles, ancient villages and city walls. Feel like a Portuguese Navigator from the Age of Discoveries and sail on the city tales and gorgeous traditional flavors.

DID YOU KNOW THAT...

Belmonte, a Castelo Branco historical village, is the birthplace of Pedro Álvares Cabral, a fearless navigator that in 1500, commanding the Portuguese Navy, sailed towards India. During the journey, and dragged by the waters, the vessels shifted their course and the crew accidentally discovered a new country – Brazil.

7 PLACES TO VISIT

1 CASTELO BRANCO SÉ CATHEDRAL
Believed to be built during the 13th or 14th centuries, the Cathedral suffered severe damage in the last quarter of the 17th century. The lack of resources for the restoration left the façade with little ornamentation.

2 CARGALEIRO MUSEUM
Devoted to one of Portugal's top artists, a creative genius of painting and ceramics – Manuel Cargaleiro.

3 JARDIM DO PAÇO EPISCOPAL (BISHOP'S PALACE GARDEN)
Laid out in the Italian style, this beautiful rectangular Baroque garden is composed of symbolic granite statues, porches, and countless lakes and fountains.

4 CENTER OF CONTEMPORARY CULTURE
Designed by the Spanish architect Josep Lluis Mateo, in joint work with the Portuguese architect Carlos Reis de Figueiredo, the center's purpose is to disseminate contemporary culture and stimulate the artistic creation.

5 PENHA GARCIA TRACE FOSSILS/PAINTED SNAKES (COBRAS PINTADAS)
These 490-million-year-old quartzite rocks hold one of the city's greatest treasures. At the time when all continents were united around the South Pole, the primitive living invertebrates that inhabited the oceans left their marks in Castelo Branco.

6 PORTAS DE RÓDÃO AND ITS CASTLE
This unique place with high geological value welcomes the Tagus river through its massive quartz rocks. The Castle of Ródão viewpoint offers a breathtaking panoramic view over the Tagus valley.

7 IDANHA-A-VELHA HISTORICAL VILLAGE
Created during the 1st century BC, the village played an essential role in transport routes between the Portuguese and Spanish cities. Due to the Roman, Visigoth, and Moor influence, its cultural heritage value is immense.

3 PLACES TO EAT

PALITÃO

Portuguese
€

This traditional restaurant offers a great Portuguese gastronomic experience. The menu isn't that varied, but it provides some delicious meat dishes. Its rustic decor resembles a farmhouse. We suggest you book in advance as there are a limited number of seats.
☎ +351 272 323 608

LENDA VIRIATO

Portuguese
€ €

If you're going north, near Covilhã, you have to visit Lenda Viriato. It's placed in a small town called Unhais da Serra right by Serra da Estrela. It's decor and clay kitchenware makes you feel like you've traveled 500 years back in time, offering a traditional and delicious Portuguese tasting experience.
☎ +351 275 971 252

CABRA PRETA

Portuguese
€ €

Cabra Preta (Black goat) proposes another take on traditional Portuguese cuisine. Placed right at the city center, the interior is very fashionable with old and new decorative twists. You shouldn't leave Castelo Branco without trying the chouriço assado – roasted pork meat sausage.
☎ +351 272 030 303

RETIRO DO CAÇADOR

Tasca

As the name suggests, Hunter's Retreat is a small, inexpensive and straightforward restaurant specializing in grilled meat including boar, rabbit, pork, and cow. We suggest their picanha, it's a pure delight – steak with white rice and black beans plus grilled vegetables and fruits.
☎ +351 239 823 790

3 PLACES TO SLEEP

HOTEL RAINHA D. AMÉLIA

★★★★
Center
A simple, yet elegant, hotel by the city center. It includes free parking spots and its staff is friendly and helpful. The breakfast quality is average.
☎ +351 272 348 800
✉ geral@hotelrainhadamelia.pt

H2OTEL

★★★★★
66KM
H2otel is another beautiful hotel near Serra da Estrela. If you're a fan of the mountain air, natural views and you're able to travel by car, you'll love this one. Great indoor Spa and pools with warm water. You'll feel renewed after a couple of days of silence and rest. We suggest you take the tour to our recommended Lenda Viriato restaurant; it's within walking distance.
☎ +351 275 330 406

TRYP COLINA DO CASTELO HOTEL

★★★★
6KM
One simple hotel option to sleep at Castelo Branco. It looks standard (last time we went there it needed some maintenance), but since it's placed at a high point, you can see Serra da Estrela and the rich natural resources around. The hotel restaurant is also recommended.
☎ +351 272 349 280

BUCKET LIST

- [ ] Take a panoramic picture from the top of Castelo Branco Castle
- [ ] Eat a regional cheese
- [ ] Take a picture at Rotunda da Europa (Europe's Roundabout)
- [ ] Check out the Portados Quinhentistas at the historical center (16th century door)
- [ ] Taste a Tigelada (dessert)
- [ ] Take a walk at St. Martinho Mountain
- [ ] Taste Papas de Carolo (dessert)
- [ ] Buy a Bordado Castelo Branco as a souvenir (embroidery)
- [ ] Enjoy a concert/show at Cine-Teatro Avenida
- [ ] Find a Viola Beiroa player (typical guitar)
- [ ] Wander Belmonte streets (historical village)
- [ ] Have lunch at Petiscos & Granitos rock restaurant (Monsanto)
- [ ] Take a pedestrian trail at NaturTejo Geopark
- [ ] Go to the Schist Village of Castelo Novo and find out where the gallows were placed
- [ ] Try Azeite da Beira Baixa (olive oil) with broa (traditional bread)

SPECIAL DATES

- Romaria de Nossa Senhora de Mércoles (2nd Sunday after Easter)
- Templar days of Castelo Branco (end of May/beginning of June)
- Bienal do Azeite, Olive Oil Festival (even years)

SHOPPING

- Forum Castelo Branco – Avenida Professor Doutor Egas Moniz
- Avenida Primeiro de Maio

HOW TO GET TO

🚗 CAR
Porto: 🕐2h30 🛣️A1, IC8
Lisboa: 🕐2h15 🛣️A1, A23

🚆 TRAIN
Porto: 🕐4h30 🚆IC ➡ Castelo Branco
Lisboa: 🕐2h45 🚆IC ➡ Castelo Branco

🚌 BUS
Porto: 🕐5h00
Lisboa: 🕐3h00

ℹ️ CITY TRANSPORTATION
Bus: TUCAB
www.tucab.transdev.pt/horarios

PRICE RATING

89

LEIRIA

This adventurous city, marked by battles, conquests and kings, is the ideal place to rest from the big cities. Discover the urban legends together with the fantastic and noble Leiria architecture. Be dazzled by the green forests and incredible beaches and allow yourself to be immersed in some of the most significant Portuguese novels.

DID YOU KNOW THAT...

A ALA DOS NAMORADOS

Back in the 14th century, the Spaniards were forcing themselves into Leiria in another attempt to conquer the Portuguese territory. During the invasion, Brites de Almeida became a legend and a national heroine for killing seven Spanish soldiers with her baker's shovel. The Aljubarrota Battle immortalized this unique and fearless figure – the Aljubarrota Baker.

7 PLACES TO VISIT

1 LEIRIA CASTLE
Raised under the order of D. Afonso Henriques (First King of Portugal) as a defensive line against the Moors, the well-preserved castle houses a variety of historical points of interest inside: the Church of Nossa Senhora da Pena, the former Royal Palace, and the Keep.

2 MERCADO S'ANTANA
Designed by the Swiss architect Ernesto Korrodi in the 1920's, the former market later became a well-respected Cultural Center. The building promotes a wide range of exciting events and accommodates the Theatre of Miguel Franco.

3 LEIRIA SÉ CATHEDRAL
Dated from the 16th century, this sober building of Mannerist characteristics stands out for its altarpiece paintings, allusive to the life of the Virgin Mary, and the two large-scale organs in Baroque style.

4 CHAPEL OF NOSSA SENHORA DA ENCARNAÇÃO
On the hilltop of St. Gabriel Mount lays this Catholic place of pilgrimage and devotion. Built in the late 16th century, it is known for its grand staircase, tiles, and paintings allusive to the life of the Blessed Virgin.

5 LEIRIA MUSEUM, ST. AGOSTINHO CONVENT
Built over the St. Agostinho Convent, the Museum compiles a collection of artifacts related to the city, telling its story in a surprising way.

6 BATALHA MONASTERY (BATALHA)
One of the most fascinating Gothic monuments in the Iberian Peninsula, this Monastery is a sign of gratitude to the Virgin Mary, upon Her active intervention with the war against the Castilians.

7 MIRA DE AIRE CAVES (PORTO DE MÓS)
These set of limestone caves, which straddles over 11 kilometers, is considered a wonder of nature. Opened to the public in 1974, its environmental value attracts the curiosity of speleologists and tourists on a regular basis.

3 PLACES TO EAT

CASINHA VELHA

Portuguese

€ € €

A family-run restaurant with a cozy atmosphere with rustic and regionally inspired decor. Delicious home cooking accompanied by an extensive and interesting wine list.

📞 +351 244 855 355

PANGEIA RESTAURANTE

Mediterranean

€ €

Placed at the world-known surf spot, Nazaré, this restaurant will make your trip worth it. The service is top-notch, and the menus are rich, especially the octopus.

The outdoor area offers a garden and a terrace with a superb view over the town of Nazaré and the Atlantic Ocean.

📞 +351 917 934 726

TROMBA RIJA

Portuguese

€ €

Tromba Rija is a small, old-fashioned tavern that opened more than 50 years ago. It offers a diverse, self-service all-you-can-eat buffet. It includes 30+ starters and a lot of delicious desserts.

📞 +351 244 852 277

TASCA 7

Tasca

This old tasca is loved by the locals. Tasca 7 doesn't have a static menu, and its entrance can be found only by searching for the number 7 that gives it the name.

The most popular snacks are the codfish cakes, pig's ear, octopus

---

salad and many simple tidbits that will make you feel part of the cook's family.

📞 +351 239 823 790

3 PLACES TO SLEEP

TRYP LEIRIA HOTEL

⭐⭐⭐⭐
1KM

Tryp hotel is the best option to stay in the center of Leiria. With great road access and within walking distance from the center, it's a recently built, modern looking and comfortable hotel. It doesn't have a swimming pool, so you'll have to rely on the beach for an open-air bath.

📞 +351 244 249 900
✉ tryp.leiria@meliaportugal.com

HOTEL VILLA BATALHA

⭐⭐⭐⭐
14KM

This hotel sits at the side of an imposing monastery that shares its name. The interior receives excellent natural daylight, the public areas are broad, and the panoramic balconies welcome you to overlook the nearby mountains.

Here you'll also find well-equipped rooms, a Spa, and interior swimming pool.

📞 +351 244 240 400
✉ geral@hotelvillabatalha.pt

LISOTEL HOTEL & SPA

⭐⭐⭐⭐
9KM

A themed hotel by the entrance of Leiria with 32 rooms distinguished by 7 different motifs that stand for love stories. It includes a great-looking and relaxing Spa and an amazingly innovative interior pool.

📞 +351 244 820 460

BUCKET LIST ✓

- ☐ Take a picture at the top of St. Bartolomeu Mount (Nazaré)
- ☐ Drink a shot of Ginjinha in a chocolate cup (Óbidos)
- ☐ Run through the Pinhal de Leiria pine forest
- ☐ Eat Broas de Batata Doce (pastry)
- ☐ Take the route O Crime do Padre Amaro (urban art)
- ☐ Go to Peniche for seabird watching
- ☐ Take the boat to Berlengas (islands) and check out St. João Baptista Fortress
- ☐ Check out D. Pedro and D. Inês de Castro's sculpted tombs at Alcobaça Monastery
- ☐ Take the route Os Escritores em Leiria (historic buildings)
- ☐ Try a nautical sport at Figueira da Foz beach
- ☐ Bathe in Lagoa da Ervideira (lagoon)
- ☐ Have a snack at Nut'Leiria
- ☐ Eat Brisas do Lis (pastry)
- ☐ Look for the oldest piece of art at Museum of Glass (Marinha Grande)
- ☐ Find someone handcrafting a wicker basket

SPECIAL DATES ★

- Torres Vedras Carnival (February)
- City Day (May 22nd – Municipal Holiday)
- May Fair (May)
- Santa Cruz Ocean Spirit in Torres Vedras – Surf Competition (July)
- Óbidos Mercado Medieval, Medieval Fair (July – August)
- Entremuralhas Summer Festival (August)

SHOPPING

- Leiria Shopping – Rua do Alto Vieiro
- Rua Barão de Viamonte

HOW TO GET TO

🚗 CAR
Porto: 🕐1h45 🛣A1
Lisboa: 🕐1h30 🛣A1

🚆 TRAIN
Porto: 🕐2h30 🚄AP ⮕ Coimbra-B ⇄ IR ⮕ Leiria
Lisboa: 🕐3h30 🚄AP ⮕ Coimbra-B ⇄ R ⮕ Amieira ⇄ R ⮕ Leiria

🚌 BUS
Porto: 🕐2h30
Lisboa: 🕐2h00

ℹ CITY TRANSPORTATION
Bus: Mobilis – www.mobilis.pt

PRICE RATING €

PORTALEGRE

The singular landscape of the imposing Portalegre owns an exquisite collection of magnificent medieval fragments. Thrill yourself with the spectacular concentration of mercantile mansions and the fabulous examples of religious architecture. Enjoy the gorgeous hilltop towns and villages and lose yourself in the twisting cobbled streets of Alto Alentejo's Capital.

DID YOU KNOW THAT...

In Marvão village it is possible to see the backs of the birds flying by. This statement, commonly used by the locals, may well be right as the Castle stands at such a height (around 860 meters) that it makes you feel like you're in Heaven.

7 PLACES TO VISIT

1 PORTALEGRE SÉ CATHEDRAL
Dated from 1556, this renaissance and baroque style church houses a unique collection of Mannerist paintings. The incredible works of art of Portuguese artists from the 16th and 17th centuries ascend to over 90.

2 ST. BERNARDO MONASTERY
Founded in the early 16th century by the archbishop D. Jorge de Melo, its primary purpose at the time was housing damsels with no dowry. The sumptuous grave of D. Jorge and the 18th century tiles panels are true relics.

3 ROBINSON'S FACTORY MUSEUM (CORK)
This centenary former factory is an excellent place to learn a bit more about one of the Portuguese ex-libris: the cork. At the museum, the cork's transformation is explained in detail; its types and practical applications.

4 SÃO MAMEDE NATURAL PARK
A protected green area contrasting with the arid and dry landscapes of the Alentejo. The perfect place to take pedestrian trails, watch rare birds of prey and observe historical heritage.

5 PORTALEGRE GUY FINO MUSEUM (TAPESTRY)
The former Castelo-Branco residence displays a brilliant and expensive collection of tapestries from some of the most renowned national and international authors of the sector.

6 PORTALEGRE CASTLE
In dominant position over the city, this 13th century Castle was part of the Portuguese defensive system. Inside the monument there is a military museum, exhibiting armory pieces from the 15th century to the First World War.

7 CASTELO DE VIDE AND MARVÃO MEDIEVAL VILLAGES
A cultural heritage treasure endowed with castles and historical monuments. While Castelo de Vide grants one of the most important examples of the Jewish presence in Portugal, Marvão offers an astonishing view from the highest crest of the Serra de São Mamede.

95

3 PLACES TO EAT

RESTAURANTE SOLAR DO FORCADO

Portuguese

€ €

Located on a cobblestone street in the historic center by the castle, Solar do Forcado presents rustic decor themed around the tourada – bullfighting. The menu is diverse and meat-oriented, which we suggest accompanying with a quality red wine from the Alentejo.

📞 +351 249 531 633

RESTAURANTE POEIRAS

Portuguese

€ €

A good offering of local cuisine enhanced by a substantial wine list. With a central location, you'll find it hidden behind a glass façade.
The roasted duck rice is a must!

📞 +351 245 201 862

ACONTECE RESTAURANTE

Mediterranean

€ €

If you choose to get to know Elvas and its marvelous fortress, you should try Acontece (which means Happening). It offers a youthful ambiance supported by background music, modern decor with intelligently placed items and remarkable service.

📞 +351 969 880 660

NA BOCA DO LOBO

Tasca

A special tasca run by Chef José Júlio Vintém. Merging the gourmet with the traditional Alentejan cuisine, you'll get some of the best tidbits of the region: salted bacon with garlic, roasted pork belly/chicken or even some frog legs.
Placed right at the city's heart, it's an interesting and inexpensive alternative to the traditional restaurant.

📞 +351 965 416 630

 # 3 PLACES TO SLEEP

ROSSIO HOTEL

⭐⭐⭐⭐

Center

It's quite small in size, but the rooms are large enough and quite enjoyable. It's recently built, so the decor is modern and matches the Alentejan region spirit.

📞 +351 245 082 218

✉ geral@rossiohotel.com

HOTEL CONVENTO D'ALTER

⭐⭐⭐⭐

27KM

Placed at Alter do Chão village, the hotel emerged from the restoration of an old Franciscan convent from the 16th century. The rooms and bathrooms are ample, most of them have a large balcony. The breakfast is generous, but the restaurant itself is not recommended.

📞 +351 245 619 120

✉ reservas@conventodalter.com.pt

HOTEL JOSÉ RÉGIO

⭐⭐⭐⭐

Center

Named after the Portuguese writer José Maria dos Reis Pereira, pen name José Régio, who lived most of his life in Portalegre, its central theme revolves around Régio's poetry. This hotel offers 35 rooms and a cafeteria that exhibits the passion of this writer in every corner. The city center is at 5 minutes walking distance.

📞 +351 245 009 190

✉ info@hoteljoseregio.com

BUCKET LIST

- [ ] Take the Senhora da Lapa pedestrian trail
- [ ] Taste Toucinho-do-Céu (desert)
- [ ] Find a Portalegre typical wicker basket
- [ ] Visit the Serra de São Mamede for bird watching
- [ ] Watch someone playing Pandeiro de Portalegre (tambourine)
- [ ] Cross the three city doors: Devesa, Alegrete, and Crato
- [ ] Check out Rossio's giant and ancient Plane Tree
- [ ] Buy a cork souvenir
- [ ] Taste Rebuçados de ovo de Portalegre (pastry)
- [ ] Go for a wine tasting at Adega de Portalegre (wine cellar)
- [ ] Learn the name of the Seven Convents from a local
- [ ] Watch the landscape from the top of the Nossa Senhora da Graça Fortress (Elvas)
- [ ] Cross the border to Spain at Elvas
- [ ] Ride a Lusitano horse at Alter do Chão
- [ ] Watch the Tagus river from the Castle of Belver (Gavião)

SPECIAL DATES

- Jazzfest – Jazz Festival (March)
- Conventual sweets' Fair (April)
- Festa dos Aventais – The Aprons Festival (May)
- City Festival (May 23rd – Municipal Holiday)
- Feira das Cebolas – Onions' Fair (September)
- Baja 500 Portalegre – FIA championship (October)

SHOPPING

- Centro Comercial Fontedeira – Avenida Movimento das Forças Armadas, 33
- Centro Comercial Continente de Portalegre – Rua do Joinal, 12
- Rua 5 de Outubro

HOW TO GET TO

CAR

Porto: 3h00 A1, A13, IC8, A23, IP2
Lisboa: 2h30 A2, A6, E802

TRAIN

Porto: 4h30 AP Entroncamento R Portalegre
Lisboa: 4h00 AP Entroncamento R Portalegre

BUS

Porto: 7h00
Lisboa: 3h00

CITY TRANSPORTATION

Bus: SMAT Transportes – https://foxhoundglobal.com/yourls/8np3a

PRICE RATING

€ € € € €

LISBOA AND THE TAGUS VALLEY

LISBOA

This captivating and cosmopolitan city, which inspired artists for centuries, is considered one of the most exciting metropoles in Europe. Immerse in Lisboa's tremendous opulence and elegance, where history and modern life go hand in hand. Feel the exceptional natural light and breathe the cultural diversity of the graceful, yet extravagant, bourgeois of Portugal's Capital.

DID YOU KNOW THAT...

Once a year, in September, an underpass is open on Rua da Prata which leads to the so-called Roman Galleries. This Cryptoporticus, discovered after the Lisboa earthquake in 1755 emanates mystery through its tunnels, narrow corridors, water avenues and low passages.

10 PLACES TO VISIT

1 JERÓNIMOS MONASTERY
A real example of the Portuguese wealth in the 15th century. Attention is inevitably drawn to the façades, the Church, and the Cloisters. The mortal remains of great Portuguese poets, Navigators, and Kings can be found inside the main church.

2 BELÉM TOWER
This defense Tower, ordered to be built by King Manuel I, symbolizes the proximity of the country to the ocean and the maritime discoveries of new worlds. The royal coat of arms, the armillary sphere, and the cross of the Order of Christ arise as a lasting symbol of King Manuel I's mighty reign.

3 MONUMENT TO THE DISCOVERIES
An imposing monument dedicated to the Portuguese explorers during the Discoveries period. Constituted by a caravel, headed by the figure of Prince Henrique, followed by a cortege of 32 important and essential navigators from the epoch.

4 PANTEÃO NACIONAL
It honors and perpetuates the memory of Portuguese citizens who have distinguished themselves for services rendered to the country, such as singers, football players, writers, and politicians.

5 ST. JORGE CASTLE
Situated on the highest hilltop of the city, it is known for its majestic and luxurious landscapes. The museum inside this ancient fortification from the 2nd century BC presents the history of Lisboa.

6 PRAÇA DO COMÉRCIO/TERREIRO DO PAÇO
One of the biggest, fanciest squares in Europe, it is an entrance to a variety of exciting spots of the city. The King José I statue, sculpted by Machado de Castro, perfectly illustrates the royal power and the nobility of the Lusitano horse.

7 PARQUE DAS NAÇÕES
The Expo 98 former venue is a unique leisure area in the country, combining water and green spaces. A 5-kilometer-long architectural masterpiece by the Tagus River.

8 NATIONAL ANCIENT ART MUSEUM
The most relevant public artifacts, from the 12th to the 19th centuries, incorporate the collection of the Museum. There are endless Portuguese, European, African and Oriental works of art as paintings, sculptures, silver, gold, jewelry and decoration motifs.

101

9 EDUARDO VII PARK

This 25-hectare leisure space in the heart of Lisboa offers a privileged view over the city. The Park is enriched by multiple exotic plant species and flanked by long walks of Calçada Portuguesa. The Sports' Pavilion – Pavilhão Carlos Lopes – is located in the east wing.

10 PALACE OF PENA (SINTRA)

The Palace of Pena is considered one of the most prominent examples of Portuguese Romanticism in the 19th century. In addition to this fairytale royal summer palace, the National Park also preserves the most astonishing collection of camellias in Portugal.

⑂ 7 PLACES TO EAT

BELCANTO
Mediterranean
€ € €

Belcanto opened in 1958 in Chiado – Bairro Alto, and its excellence was distinguished by two Michelin stars. In the attractive dining room, renovated in a classical yet simplistic style, the sophisticated menus are the art of the renowned chef José Avillez. Ring the bell to enter.
📞 +351 213 420 607

FRADE DOS MARES
Seafood
€ €

Tucked away in a street corner of Av. Dom Carlos, Frade dos Mares is a bit away from the tourist whirl.
It provides a vivid offer of seafood such as octopus (Polvo à Lagareiro) and codfish. Excellent price-quality ratio.
📞 +351 213 909 418

FEITORIA
Mediterranean
€ € €

Inside Altis Belém Hotel & SPA you'll find this Michelin-starred restaurant.
Chef João Rodrigues focuses his dishes and menus on national products and in the defense of sustainability and the natural cycles of nature.
📞 +351 210 400 208

LOCO RESTAURANTE
Mediterranean
€ €

Loco is a Michelin-starred restaurant located next to the Basílica da Estrela. Chef Alexandre Silva, who won the Portuguese cuisine competition, Top Chef, will guide you through an incredible gastronomic experience. There are two menus to choose from: Discover (introductory) and Loco (full menu).
📞 +351 213 951 861

LISBOA WINERY
Winery
€ €

Although this area is supposed to be about eating, we couldn't help but mention Lisboa Winery. It's a tasting center and wine bar in Bairro Alto that has a unique environment and a premium collection of Portuguese wines served by the glass.
Enjoy the olive oil tasting and cheese/meat board for the full experience.
📞 +351 218 260 132

TABERNA DA RUA DAS FLORES
Tasca

Born from an old grocery store,

Taberna da Rua das Flores recovers the somewhat lost spirit of the real Portuguese tasca. With few seats and minimal decoration to follow the tradition, here you'll find great regional wine, and a variety of meal offers, from sausages to cheeses, codfish, clams and fresh tuna.

📞 +351 213 479 418

MAÇÃ VERDE
Tasca

Maça verde (green apple) is the locals' choice for a quick, delicious and inexpensive meal. They offer a variety of fresh fish, good wine, and very well-made codfish. You might have a hard time finding the modest façade, but the service will make up for it.

📞 +351 965 512 266

5 PLACES TO SLEEP

VALVERDE HOTEL
⭐⭐⭐⭐⭐
Center

Located at the city center – Avenida da Liberdade, this luxurious boutique hotel boasts contemporary furniture, artwork, and antiques. With a small number of rooms, it presents itself as an exclusive option to be surrounded by the beauty of Lisboa.

📞 +351 210 940 300
✉ info@valverdehotel.com

HERITAGE AVENIDA LIBERDADE
⭐⭐⭐⭐
Center

Heritage was born in a refurbished building from the 18th century at the heart of Lisboa. With a cosmopolitan and charming decoration by the architect Miguel Câncio Martins and an attractive blue façade, it provides

medium-sized rooms and a delicious buffet breakfast.

📞 +351 234 401 000
✉ melia.ria@meliaportugal.com

PENHA LONGA RESORT
⭐⭐⭐⭐⭐
30KM

If you're seeking a more natural, green place to stay, you should definitely try this resort. Penha Longa is an elegant and relaxed estate situated by the Sintra Natural Reserve Hills, just 12km away from the gorgeous Palace of Pena. Being a Ritz-Carlton Hotel, it has great service and infrastructure with a beautiful outdoor swimming pool, combined with a Michelin-starred restaurant.

📞 +351 234 067 063
✉ penhalonga@penhalonga.com

HOTEL CASCAIS MIRAGEM
⭐⭐⭐⭐⭐
1KM

Placed just 3km from the Cascais center, this luxurious hotel resides at the beachside, providing a magnificent vista over the seaside setting. Boasting a modern and rich decoration with a relaxed environment, it includes an infinity pool, spacious rooms with a lovely balcony, an SPA, and generous breakfasts.

📞 +351 210 060 600
✉ reservations@cascaismirage.com

INTERCONTINENTAL ESTORIL
⭐⭐⭐⭐⭐
27KM

Another outstanding option to stay outside the Lisboa center. Located near the famous Casino Estoril and Cascais city, the InterContinental Estoril has a privileged location on the waterfront.

With a noticeable luxury feel and professional service, we advise you to ask for the rooms with the ocean view (third floor).

📞 +351 218 291 100
✉ liset.reservations@ihg.com

SPECIAL DATES

- Lisboa Fashion Week (March and October)
- Lisboa Fish & Flavours, food festival (April)
- Estoril Open, ATP World Tour – Estoril (April/May)
- Rock in Rio (May – biannual)
- Alkantara Festival (May)
- St. António Festival (June 13th – Municipal Holiday)
- Super Bock Super Rock Music Festival (July)
- NOS Alive Music Festival (July)

HOW TO GET TO

🚗 CAR
Porto: 🕐 3h00 🛣️ A1

🚆 TRAIN
Porto: 🕐 3h00 🚈 AP ➲ Lisboa

🚇 METRO
Aeroporto station: 🕐 0h30 🚈 Red line ➲ São Sebastião station 🚈 Green line ➲ Santa Apolónia station (leave in Baixa – Chiado station)

🚌 BUS
Porto: 🕐 3h30

ℹ️ CITY TRANSPORTATION
Bus: Carris – www.carris.pt
Metro: Metropolitano de Lisboa – www.metrolisboa.pt
Train: CP – www.cp.pt

SHOPPING

- Centro Comercial Colombo – Avenida Lusíada
- Centro Vasco da Gama – Avenida Dom João II, 40
- Amoreiras Shopping Center – Avenida Engenheiro Duarte Pacheco, 2037
- Avenida da Liberdade
- Rua Augusta
- Chiado

AREAS TO AVOID

- Chelas
- Picheleira
- Damaia
- Quinta das Conchas

PRICE RATING

BUCKET LIST ✓

- [ ] Take the city's famous elevators: Santa Justa, Bica, and Ascensor da Glória
- [ ] Taste a Pastel de Belém (pastry)
- [ ] Take a walk by the river at Terreiro do Paço
- [ ] Take a picture with the Fernando Pessoa statue at Chiado
- [ ] Observe Lisboa in 360° looking through the periscope of the Torro do Tombo
- [ ] Visit the Royal Convent and Palace of Mafra
- [ ] Have dinner in Bairro Alto
- [ ] Appreciate the fauna and flora of the five oceans at the Oceanarium
- [ ] Enjoy a breathtaking view over the Parque das Nações and the Tagus river riding the cable car.
- [ ] Buy a souvenir at Feira da Ladra
- [ ] Check out the view from Senhora do Monte viewpoint
- [ ] Learn the Tile's history at the National Tile Museum
- [ ] Listen to Fado Vadio, or amateur, in the Alfama, Mouraria or Madragoa neighborhoods
- [ ] Climb to the top of Rua Augusta Arch
- [ ] Check out the outstanding coaches' collection at the National Coach Museum
- [ ] Take a tram ride through the historic neighborhoods
- [ ] Spend a day at the Lisboa Zoo
- [ ] Cross the Tagus River by boat
- [ ] Live the Experience Pilar 7 at the Ponte 25 de Abril (Avenida da Índia).
- [ ] Take a look at the creativity displayed in the LXFACTORY Sunday Market (Rua Rodrigues de Faria)

SANTARÉM

Full of personality and green hills, it is considered the second Portuguese beauty, placed after Minho. Santarém, the Impregnable City, preserves numerous castles and walls that rank it amongst the most historical cities in the country. Spirituality floats in the air, as the religious tourism attracts millions of pilgrims to Fátima – the Portuguese Mecca.

DID YOU KNOW THAT...

Faithful servants abiding by a strict religious discipline and skilled soldiers, the Templars enjoyed great prestige when they entered the Portuguese territory. Brave and feared, lords of an enviable wealth, these Knights were a fundamental piece in the Christian Reconquest. After assisting D. Afonso Henriques in taking Santarém from the Moors, the Templars were rewarded with vast territories where they settled and built fortresses. One of these fascinating buildings is the Convent of Christ in Tomar.

7 PLACES TO VISIT

1 SANTARÉM SÉ CATHEDRAL
Located in the historical center, this 12th century Cathedral was built on the ruins of the former Royal Palace of Santarém. Its interior presents several unique decorative motifs such as gilt carvings, paintings, and sculptures.

2 PORTAS DO SOL GARDEN
Fenced by medieval walls, it offers a fantastic view over the Tagus river and the surrounding cities. The ideal place for rest and enjoying the historic environment.

3 DIOCESANO MUSEUM
Adjacent to the Santarém Sé Cathedral, the Diocesano Museum exhibits an extraordinary collection of religious works of art, comprising paintings, sculptures, and other artifacts.

4 SANCTUARY OF OUR LADY OF FÁTIMA (FÁTIMA)
A place of Christian pilgrimage and Catholic devotion, preserving the memory of the events that led to its foundation – The Apparitions of Our Lady to the three little shepherds in 1917. Its magnitude and relevance from the religious point of view have long been widely recognized.

5 CONVENT OF CHRIST IN TOMAR (UNESCO W.H.)
A set of historic buildings (Castle, Templar Charola, Cloisters, Manueline church, Renaissance convent, among others) whose construction dates to 1160. It is closely linked to the beginnings of the Kingdom of Portugal and to the role of the Order of the Templars.

6 ALMOUROL CASTLE (VILA NOVA DA BARQUINHA)
Standing on a granite outcrop, on a small island of 310 meters long by 75 meters wide, the Castle is one of the most representative examples of military architecture.

7 OURÉM CASTLE
Built in the 15th century, it is another appealing military architectural work. Although its structure was severely damaged by the earthquake of 1755 and the Peninsular War (1807–1814), the restoration works in the early 1900's have kept its glory intact these days.

3 PLACES TO EAT

RESTAURANTE A GRELHA
Portuguese
€

Even though the exterior isn't that appealing, this restaurant has great fresh fish, octopus, and grilled food menus.
Don't forget to make a reservation, especially on weekends.
📞 +351 249 531 633

PIGALLE
Seafood
€ €

A small, lovely restaurant with a clean and irreverent decoration. It offers delicious food and eye-catching plate presentation.
The octopus salad is divine.
📞 +351 243 046 865

ADIAFA
Portuguese
€ €

Adiafa is one of the oldest restaurants in Santarém, situated near the city market. Its large room decor is pretty outdated, but the gastronomic proposals are genuine and well-made. Providing a great variety of fresh fish and some attractive meat alternatives, we suggest the mangusto with codfish, which is made of cabbage, potatoes, olive oil, salt, and garlic.
📞 +351 912 378 869

TABERNA Ó BALCÃO
Tasca

This small restaurant tries to simulate an old bullfight arena tavern with retro design elements and paintings. It focuses on more straightforward dishes, but offers a multitude of iconic Portuguese treats.
📞 +351 243 055 883

3 PLACES TO SLEEP

SANTARÉM HOTEL
⭐⭐⭐⭐
1KM

The only viable hotel option in Santarém city will allow you to enjoy the famous Lezíria (highly fertile grounds) and the Tagus River. Located in a calm city area, you can take a 20-minute walk to the city center. Room comfort is average, and the decoration is quite outdated.
📞 +351 243 330 800
✉ geral@santaremhotel.net

HOTEL DOS TEMPLÁRIOS
⭐⭐⭐⭐
66KM

Hotel dos Templários has a privileged location in the city center of Tomar. Surrounded by majestic gardens and overlooking the Nabão river, it offers a relaxed environment and a comfortable stay without the hustle and bustle of the big cities.
📞 +351 249 310 100
✉ geral@hoteldostemplarios.pt

HOTEL ANJO DE PORTUGAL
⭐⭐⭐⭐
56KM

Anjo de Portugal creates a clean, minimalist design to match the spirituality of the nearby world-famous Shrine of Fátima. Here you'll have a calm stay with high-quality rooms and free parking. Breakfast is average.
📞 +351 244 820 460
✉ reservas@hotelanjodeportugal.pt

BUCKET LIST ✓

- ☐ Try an Adega do Cartaxo wine (wine cellar)
- ☐ Watch a traditional bullfight
- ☐ Check out Pedro Álvares Cabral tomb (discoverer of Brazil) at Igreja da Graça
- ☐ Buy a Fátima souvenir
- ☐ Take the Dinosaur footprints pedestrian trail at Serra de Aire (Ourém)
- ☐ Learn how to make paper flowers for Festival dos Tabuleiros (Tomar)
- ☐ Try Sopa de Pedra (stone soup) at Almeirim
- ☐ Visit the biggest subterranean room in the country – Algar do Pena Cave
- ☐ Take a panoramic picture from Portas do Sol viewpoint
- ☐ Take the Marinhas de Sal pedestrian trail at Serra dos Candeeiros (Rio Maior)
- ☐ Check out the megalithic tomb at Alcobertas (Rio Maior)
- ☐ Eat Pampilhos (pastry)
- ☐ Take a picture with a Forcado (bull face catcher)
- ☐ Buy fresh biological foods at Mercado Municipal (Old Square)
- ☐ Check out the tiles at St. Maria de Marvila Church

SPECIAL DATES ★

- St. José Festival (March 19th – Municipal Holiday)
- Religious Celebrations at Fátima (May 13th)
- National Agricultural Fair (June)
- National Gastronomy Festival (October)
- Golegã Equestrian Fair (November)

SHOPPING

- W Shopping – Rua Pedro de Santarém, 29
- Rua Capelo e Ivens

HOW TO GET TO

🚗 CAR
Porto: 🕐2h15 🛣A1
Lisboa: 🕐1h00 🛣A1

🚆 TRAIN
Porto: 🕐2h15 🚆AP ➡ Santarém
Lisboa: 🕐0h45 🚆IC ➡ Santarém

🚌 BUS
Porto: 🕐3h00
Lisboa: 🕐1h00

ℹ CITY TRANSPORTATION
Bus: Scalabus – www.scalabus.pt
Rodoviária do Tejo – www.rodotejo.pt

PRICE RATING €

€ € € € €

SETÚBAL

Be delighted with the magnificent diversity and quality of the Setúbal Peninsula. This unique region, blessed by Mother Nature, was rewarded with refined and balanced wines and terrific natural assets, such as its enviable beaches and incomparable beautiful landscapes. Setúbal blends the perfect ingredients to create the most pleasurable experience: mountain, river, sea, culture, and gastronomy.

DID YOU KNOW THAT...

Eight-hundred and twenty feet from the marvelous Portinho's Beach there's this curious rock islander called Pedra da Anicha. The rock is part of Arrábida Nature Reserve and its abundant submerged aquatic vegetation, together with its surrounding sand bed, are responsible for sheltering more than 70 species and marine invertebrates.

7 PLACES TO VISIT

1 SERRA DA ARRÁBIDA (MOUNTAIN)
The Mountain provides one of the most stunning coastal scenarios in the Lisboa region. It is also the perfect site to exercise and get in shape by trying one of the various available activities such as hiking, cycling or orientation programs.

2 THE CONVENT OF JESUS
The project was born in the late 15th century, aiming to collect a group of Franciscan nuns from the Order of Saint Claire. Its primary features include the church façade, the entrance, and the windows that signalize the beginning of the Portuguese Manueline style.

3 TRÓIA PENINSULA
The peninsula, on the south side of the River Sado, is a tourist resort with 18km of sandy beaches and plenty of attractions. Besides the glamour of the fancy zones, there are also some places worth visiting, such as the Roman ruins or the Carrasqueira Harbor.

4 SHRINE OF NOSSA SENHORA DO CABO
The Shrine was built during peacetime in the 18th century. In its interior, there are carefully crafted pieces of invaluable artistic value, such as the baroque main altar, the ceiling painted in perspective or the paintings allusive to St. Tiago and St. António.

5 SESIMBRA CASTLE
The last well-preserved Castle over the sea. Dated from the 9th century, today the monument is the stage for numerous cultural initiatives. Besides the permanent exhibitions, the Castle offers an autonomous historical circuit for tourists.

6 THE LABOR MUSEUM OF MICHEL GIACOMETTI
Located in the old fish canning factory, Perienes Lda. the museum studies, preserves and disseminates techniques and know-how related to the evolution of work within the community.

7 MOINHO DE MARÉ DA MOURISCA (MILL)
Built initially for cereal grinding and flour production, the Mill is now an interactive center.

3 PLACES TO EAT

PÉROLA DA MOURISCA

Mediterranean

€ €

Placed by the Herdade da Mourisca and its mill, around 9km from Setubal's center, Pérola da Mourisca offers an excellent choice of seafood, shellfish, and regional dishes.

Within its simple and pleasant facilities, you'll find some of the highest flavors of the Sado river.

📞 +351 265 793 689

CASA MATEUS

Mediterranean

€ € €

If you pass by Sesimbra, you shouldn't skip Casa Mateus. Outside you'll find the charming and traditional Portuguese tiles. The menu offers a selection of conventional Portuguese seafood dishes, prepared exquisitely. We highly recommend the shellfish rice.

📞 +351 963 650 939

OSTRADOMUS

Seafood

€ €

A simply furnished restaurant that serves traditional cuisine with a particular focus on shellfish. There is also a good choice of tapas, as well as oysters from the restaurant's own oyster farm, hence its name OSTRAdomus (Ostra means oyster).

📞 +351 936 450 475

LEO DOS PETISCOS

Tasca

If you visit Setubal, you can't leave without trying the city's most eaten meal: chocos fritos (fried cuttlefish). It's a very simple recipe that Leo

dos Petiscos does marvelously: crunchy, well-fried and tasty.

📞 +351 239 823 790

3 PLACES TO SLEEP

NOVOTEL SETÚBAL

★ ★ ★ ★ ★

3KM

This nature-themed hotel is just at the entrance of the city. Although the room design and furniture are a bit outdated, it's a good option if you have your own means of transportation.

📞 +351 265 739 370

TRÓIA DESIGN HOTEL

★ ★ ★ ★ ★

5KM

Surrounded by sea, mountain, and beach, this area provides a panoramic view of Setubal's natural resources. Regarding the hotel itself, it's what you would expect from a 5-star resort, which includes a marvelous casino and two restaurants.

📞 +351 265 498 000

HOTEL CASA DA PALMELA

★ ★ ★ ★ ★

6KM

Situated in the heart of Serra da Arrábida, you'll find a restored house from the 17th century surrounded by beautiful vineyards. This natural environment will allow you to relax and enjoy a quiet stay, accompanied by the historic elements and charming traditional decor.

📞 +351 265 249 650

✉ reservations-casapalmela@ouh.pt

⚠ AREAS TO AVOID

- Bairro da Bela Vista
- Quinta da Princesa (Seixal)
- Bairro Branco (Almada)

BUCKET LIST

- ☐ Cross the Sado River to Tróia peninsula in a Ferry-boat
- ☐ Check out the fresh fish at Livramento's Market
- ☐ Taste the famous Moscatel of Setúbal (wine)
- ☐ Take a dip at Portinho's Beach (Serra da Arrábida)
- ☐ Eat canned sardines
- ☐ Go to Bocage Statue, and ask a local to crack a joke about him
- ☐ Watch the flamingos at Mouriscas' Tidal Mill (Herdade da Mourisca, Faralhão)
- ☐ Taste Tortas do Cego in Azeitão (pastry)
- ☐ Cross Avenida José Mourinho, named for the world-known football coach
- ☐ Have lunch at the fishing neighborhoods Fontainhas or Troino
- ☐ Taste Chocos fritos (fried cuttlefish)
- ☐ Watch the dolphins at Sado Estuary Nature Reserve
- ☐ Photograph The Boy with the Birds (street art from Sérgio Odeith)
- ☐ Go for a walk at Albarquel Urban Park
- ☐ Check out the Chapel at Lapa de Santa Margarida Cave

SPECIAL DATES

- Sant'Iago Fair (late July, early August)
- Marisco no Largo Food Festival (August)
- Avante Festival in Atalaia (September)
- The Grape Harvest Festival in Palmela (September)
- Bocage and City Day (September 15th – Municipal Holiday)

SHOPPING

- Alegro Setúbal – Av. Antero de Quental, 2
- Atlantic Park Setúbal – Avenida Mestre Lima Freitas
- Centro Comercial do Bonfim – Avenida República da Guiné Bissau,30
- Setúbal historical center and downtown streets

HOW TO GET TO

🚗 CAR
Porto: 🕐3h15 🛣️A1, A12
Lisboa: 🕐1h00 🛣️A12

🚆 TRAIN
Porto: 🕐3h30 🚆AP ➡ Pinhal Novo ⇄ U ➡ Setúbal
Lisboa: 🕐1h05 🚆AP ➡ Pinhal Novo ⇄ U ➡ Setúbal

🚌 BUS
Porto: 🕐3h30
Lisboa: 🕐0h45

ℹ️ CITY TRANSPORTATION
Bus: TST – www.tsuldotejo.pt

PRICE RATING

**North
Atlantic
Ocean**

SOUTH

ÉVORA

Embrace the secret soul of Alentejo's gateway and discover its beautifully preserved medieval architecture. Delve into the past wandering Évora's narrow, winding streets, known for boasting Portuguese charm and enchantment. While this small contemporary city exudes an infectious, unhurried pace of life, the University students' liveliness creates an interesting duality.

DID YOU KNOW THAT...

Praça de Giraldo, the main city square, witnessed several Autos-de-Fé perpetrated by the Inquisition. These penance acts aimed at the public humiliation of the heretics, apostates and new Christians for non-compliance with the rules imposed by the Roman Catholic Church. Most of the time the perpetrators were burned alive at the stake to inflict fear and horror in the population.

7 PLACES TO VISIT

1 ST. FRANCISCO CHURCH (BONES' CHAPEL)
Edified in the 15th century, the Church hides an impressive Chapel filled with human skulls and bones. The primary objective of the 3 Franciscan Friars who decided to build it was to transmit the message of the transience and fragility of human life.

2 D. MANUEL PALACE PUBLIC GARDEN
The garden offers a pleasant walk through a variety of trees, plants, colorful flowerbeds and gothic ruins. The Royal Palace architecture focuses on the veranda adorned with Moorish arches in a horseshoe shape and on the twinned windows of the first floor.

3 ALMENDRES MEGALITHIC CROMLECH
Originally placed and dated from the Neolithic (4,000 BC) and Chalcolithic (2,500 BC), the monument is composed of 95 stones set in two circles. On the Summer Solstice and when positioned at the Cromlech, the Menhir of Almendres, of about 4 meters high, points to the sunrise.

4 ROMAN BATHS
Dated from the 2nd and 3rd centuries, the Roman Baths comprise three distinct areas: the Laconicum, the Praefurnium, and an outdoor pool.

5 ROMAN TEMPLE
Monument erected at the beginning of the 1st century AC, as a tribute to the Roman Emperor Augustus. After plenty of damage and modifications over time, the podium, of about 3.5 meters high and made of large blocks of granite, is almost intact.

6 ÉVORA SÉ CATHEDRAL
This fortified church of the 12th century is the most prominent cathedral in the country. The adjacent building holds a Sacred Art Museum, with particular focus on an ivory Virgin of the 13th century and the Reliquary Cross of St. Lenho.

7 ÉVORA MUSEUM
With more than 20,000 artifacts, this centenary Museum tells unending Roman, Visigoth, and Moorish stories. The highlight, however, goes to a set of 13 panels representing the Life of the Virgin.

3 PLACES TO EAT

BOTEQUIM DA MOURARIA
 Mediterranean
€ €

A tiny restaurant in the city center that presents a genuine Alentejan cuisine experience. It has only 9 seats at the counter with no reservations. The owner will guide you through the menu, which features an excellent variety of wines from the region.
📞 +351 266 746 775

DEGUST'AR
Mediterranean

€ € €

Placed in the oldest area of the M'AR De AR Aqueduto's palace, this restaurant exhibits elegant décor place below high vaulted ceilings. The gastronomic à la carte menu is centered around the cooking of the region, having Chef António Nobre's signature.

DOM JOAQUIM
 Mediterranean
€ €

Housed in a renovated building decorated with modern artwork, Dom Joaquim serves excellent traditional cuisine including lamb, pig, and dog fish in a contemporary setting.
+351 266 731 105

O LAVRADOR
Tasca

O Lavrador (The Farmer) makes terrific, big sandwiches on Alentejan bread. Its main attraction is the Lavrador toast, combining sausage, ham, cheese, and oregano.
The university students often visit the restaurant for a quick meal.
📞 +351 266 781 488

 # 3 PLACES TO SLEEP

CONVENTO DO ESPINHEIRO
★ ★ ★ ★ ★
5KM

A deluxe collection Hotel & Spa by the entrance of Évora, converted from what was a 15th century convent. A place filled with history and luxurious detail, complemented by three pools and spectacular surroundings, indulging a relaxed and spiritual experience.
📞 +351 266 788 200
✉ reservas@conventodoespinheiro.com

M'AR DE AR AQUEDUTO
★ ★ ★ ★ ★
Center

This boutique hotel is an adaptation of the 15th century Sepulveda family Palace, preserving its main architectural lines and characteristics. It's located right by the historic center, a UNESCO World Heritage site.
It boasts modern design, ample bedrooms and a view over the Roman aqueduct nearby.
📞 +351 266 740 700
✉ geral@mardearhotels.com

ALBERGARIA DO CALVÁRIO
★ ★ ★ ★
Center

A simpler alternative by Évora's city center housed in a 16th century olive oil mill. It provides 22 individually designed rooms, a cozy and inviting environment with matching service and a generous breakfast.
📞 +351 266 745 930
✉ hotel@adcevora.com

BUCKET LIST ✓

- ☐ Enjoy the view from the Alto de S. Bento viewpoint
- ☐ Cross the Porta de D. Isabel (city door)
- ☐ Take the Rota dos Vinhos do Alentejo (wine route)
- ☐ Try a water sport at Barragem do Alqueva (Dam)
- ☐ Check out the tiles at St. João Evangelista Church (Convento dos Lóios)
- ☐ Taste Alfitetes de Santa Clara (pastry)
- ☐ Take the Água da Prata pedestrian trail
- ☐ Listen to Cante Alentejano (UNESCO Intangible Cultural Heritage)
- ☐ Take a picture of the Roman Temple
- ☐ Check out the Arraiolos circular Castle
- ☐ Photograph a peacock at the public garden
- ☐ Find someone handcrafting Arraiolos Carpets
- ☐ Taste Alentejo bread baked in wood ovens
- ☐ Have a picnic at Gameiro's Ecological Park (Gameiro)
- ☐ Check out the Paleolithic paintings at Escoural Caves (Santiago do Escoural)

SPECIAL DATES

- St. João Fair (June 23rd to 1st week of July)
- St. Peter's Day (June 29th – Municipal Holiday)
- Borba Vineyard and Wine Festival (November)

SHOPPING

- Évora Plaza – Rua Luís Adelino Fonseca, Lote 4
- Praça do Giraldo

PRICE RATING

€ € € € €

HOW TO GET TO

🚗 CAR
Porto: 🕐 3h45 🛣 A1, A10, A13, A6
Lisboa: 🕐 1h30 🛣 A2, A6

🚆 TRAIN
Porto: 🕐 5h00 🚊 AP ➡ Pinhal Novo ⇌ IC ➡ Évora
Lisboa: 🕐 1h30 🚊 IC ➡ Évora

🚌 BUS
Porto: 🕐 6h00
Lisboa: 🕐 1h30

ℹ CITY TRANSPORTATION
Bus: Trevo – www.trevo.com.pt

BEJA

The city of Beja rises majestically on the Alentejan plain. Its historical richness and the magnificent gastronomic heritage transform this Oasis into an absolute must-visit. A region to discover perfect locations and live the most authentic Portuguese traditions and culture in slow motion. Feel blessed by its wild beaches and the almost untouchable nature that characterizes the Alentejo Pearl.

DID YOU KNOW THAT...

Mariana Alcoforado (1640-1723), a Portuguese nun from the Nossa Senhora da Conceição Convent in Beja, fell in love with a French cavalry officer during the Restoration War in Portugal. After Noell Bouton de Chamilly returned to France, Mariana wrote him five truthful love declarations hoping to hear from him. The Frenchman never returned the letters, to her despair. The Portuguese Letters – As Cartas Portuguesas – were published in French in 1669 and revealed the unconditional and exacerbated love of the young Mariana.

7 PLACES TO VISIT

1 BEJA CASTLE
Rebuilt in 1310, the Beja Castle is part of King Dinis' reinforcement of national defenses. Its imposing Torre de Menagem (donjon) is considered the tallest in the entire Iberian Peninsula.

2 PISÕES ROMAN VILLAGE
A villa with a collection of artifacts from the 1st century BC to the Visigoth era. Composed of over 40 rooms centered around a small peristyle.

3 MÉRTOLA CASTLE
Built upon Moorish foundations, it was considered for centuries the westernmost impregnable fortress from the Iberian Peninsula. The powerful donjon symbolizes the time that Mértola was the national headquarters of St. James' Order.

4 CONVENT OF NOSSA SENHORA DA CONCEIÇÃO AND BEJA REGIONAL MUSEUM
Founded in 1459 for a group of Claris nuns (the feminine branch of the Order of Saint Francis) this place of worship is considered one of the great examples of the late-Gothic architectural style to be found across Alentejo.

5 CHURCH OF NOSSA SENHORA DOS PRAZERES AND THE EPISCOPAL MUSEUM
Initially constructed in the 17th century, the key features include tiles and large paintings with carved woodwork frames.

6 SERPA WALLS
An imposing defensive structure made of sturdy walls. Of the 5 first doors providing access to the town only the Beja, the Moura and the Nova are still standing.

7 PARDIEIRO (ODEMIRA)
An Iron Age necropolis of eleven funeral monuments made of stone and placed side-by-side with a sub-rectangular form.

3 PLACES TO EAT

3 PLACES TO SLEEP

RESTAURANTE DOM DINIS
Portuguese
€ €

Right by the side of Beja Castle, this traditional restaurant focuses on fine meat dishes like black pork, veal, and lamb.
You should try the mixed grill accompanied by an Alentejan wine.
+351 284 324 142

HERDADE DOS GROUS RESTAURANT
Mediterranean
€ € €

Surrounded by vineyards and horse stables, this restaurant resides in the interior of a beautiful farmhouse hotel. Here you'll find some excellent Alentejan cuisine and wine produced in their own estate vineyards.
+351 284 960 000

MARISQUEIRA COSTA ALENTEJANA
Seafood
€ €

Although Alentejo is known for the meat dishes, you'll find some fresh shellfish menus at Marisqueira Costa Alentejana. Placed by the fishing village Zambujeira do Mar, you can experience splendid seafood offers, including local shrimp, octopus, and fresh fish. No reservations accepted.
+351 936 450 475

SNACK-BAR ENTRE ARCOS
Tasca

Known around Beja as Taberna do Pereira, it provides some of the best tidbits of Alentejo, being fried cachola (pork liver) one of its finest treasures.
+351 284 326 855

POUSADA CONVENTO BEJA
★ ★ ★ ★
Center

The Pousada Convento Beja is situated inside the 13th century convent of St. Francisco, by the heart of Beja's historical center. Exhibiting fine gothic architectural details and religious artifacts, this pousada provides very comfortable and personalized rooms, surrounded by peaceful gardens.
+351 218 442 001
guest@pousadas.pt

VILA GALÉ CLUBE DE CAMPO
★ ★ ★ ★
30KM

Right at the heart of Alentejo and near the Roxo dam, Vila Galé Clube de Campo offers rural and wine tourism with interesting activities to explore the natural surroundings. If you seek a peaceful environment to slow down and relax, you won't be disappointed.
+351 284 970 100
campo.reservas@vilagale.com

CASAS DA LUPA
★ ★ ★ ★ ★
124KM

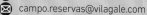

Near Zambujeira do Mar, by the coastline, Casas da Lupa contains three separate buildings surrounded by a large garden and pool. Featuring a fusion of minimalistic and rustic styles, you'll find a peaceful retreat.
+351 913 914 746
geral@casasdalupa.pt

BUCKET LIST

- [ ] Taste Trouxas-de-Ovos (pastry)
- [ ] Take the pedestrian trail Azenhas e Fortins do Guadiana (Quintos)
- [ ] Taste a regional olive oil with bread
- [ ] Cross the city on a PETRA (municipality bicycle)
- [ ] Check out the view from the Terreirinho das Peças viewpoint
- [ ] Taste Porquinhos Doces (candy)
- [ ] Have a cup of tea at Maltesinhas, an old Tea Room
- [ ] Cross the Roman bridge in Vila Ruiva (Cuba)
- [ ] Have a coffee at Café Luiz da Rocha (Mértola)
- [ ] Go to Albufeira do Roxo for birdwatching (Aljustrel)
- [ ] Try a water sport at Odivelas' Dam
- [ ] Buy a Serpa DOP traditional cheese at a local store
- [ ] Take a dip at Zambujeira do Mar beach
- [ ] Ask a local to crack a joke about alentejanos (alentejo locals)
- [ ] Take a hot air ballon ride

SPECIAL DATES

- Terras sem Sombra sacred music Festival (February to June)
- Obiveja Agricultural Fair (late April, early May)
- Dia da Espiga (May 5th – Municipal Holiday)
- International Comics' Festival (late May, early June)
- Zambujeira do Mar Meo Sudoeste Music Festival (August)
- RuralBeja Festival (October)

SHOPPING

- Rua Capitão João Francisco de Sousa
- Rua de Mértola

PRICE RATING

HOW TO GET TO

🚗 CAR
Porto: 🕔4h15 🛣A1, A10, A13, A2, A6
Lisboa: 🕔2h30 🛣A2, A6

🚆 TRAIN
Porto: 🕔5h30 🚆AP ➡ Pinhal Novo ⇄ IC ➡ Casa Branca ⇄ IC ➡ Beja
Lisboa: 🕔2h30 🚆IC ➡ Casa Branca ⇄ IC ➡ Beja

🚌 BUS
Porto: 🕔7h00
Lisboa: 🕔3h30

ℹ CITY TRANSPORTATION
Bus: TUB – URBANAS – https://foxhoundglobal.com/yours/mrkpx

FARO

Embrace the horizon as you immerse yourself in the Algarve breathtaking vistas over the ocean. The harmony between the deep blue waters and golden cliffs will absolutely light your passion. Be charmed by its gastronomic richness and the Moorish architectural influences. Feel the balance and sophistication of this distinct region – the most favored destination for the warm water and beach lovers.

DID YOU KNOW THAT...

According to the legend, Floripes, an enchanted Moor, wanders every night through the village of Olhão, seducing men and looking for the one who will free her from her spell. To break it, one man must fall in love with her and cross the Mediterranean Sea to Africa carrying a burning candle. If he succeeds marrying Floripes is the reward, but if the light blows out, the man dies and the enchantment prevails.

7 PLACES TO VISIT

1 SAGRES FORTRESS
The imposing fortification of Sagres, the westernmost point of the Iberian Peninsula, was for centuries the main war plaza of a geo-strategic maritime defensive system.

2 MEGALITHIC MONUMENTS OF ALCALAR
Ancient funerary temples built and used for several centuries in the 3rd millennium BC.

3 SILVES CASTLE
With over a thousand years, the Silves Castle is one of the most remarkable works of military architecture, inherited from the Arabs who inhabited the region.

4 ESTÓI PALACE AND ITS GARDENS
A 19th century eclectic construction considered the most significant manifestation of Romanticism in Faro district.

5 VILAMOURA MARINA
The first marina to have been built in Portugal. Highly quoted by Yacht Harbour Association and considered the best in the entire country.

6 FARO SÉ CATHEDRAL
Once a Roman Temple and a Mosque, the Sé Cathedral became a church in the 13th century. A particular note to its 18th century tube organ with chinoiserie motifs.

7 ALGARVE ETHNOGRAPHIC MUSEUM
Reconstruction of the traditional Algarve house, taverns, and markets, presenting a collection of typical regional objects and paintings.

3 PLACES TO EAT

GUSTO
Mediterranean
€ € €

Within the Conrad Hotel at Almancil, you'll find Gusto by the award-winning chef Heinz Beck, who meticulously conceives Mediterranean and international dishes. It features a lively open kitchen and an alfresco terrace with views of the infinity pool.

☎ +351 289 350 700

FAZ GOSTOS FARO
Mediterranean
€ €

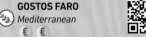

Right by the city center of Faro, Faz Gostos has two beautifully decorated dining areas, providing both gourmet and traditional Portuguese dishes.
The Morgado (almond cake) is one of the most loved desserts on the menu.

☎ +351 914 133 668

OCEAN
Mediterranean
€ € €

The Ocean Restaurant is the VILA VITA Parc Resort & Spa's fine dining signature restaurant with two Michelin Stars.
Inspired by the Atlantic Ocean, Hans Neuner Chef creates very imaginative and delightful dishes, promoting mostly seafood and Portuguese cuisine.

☎ +351 289 380 849

A TASCA DO JOÃO
Tasca

This tasca is a wonderful place to enjoy the true essence of traditional Portugal tapas and cuisine, without being tampered by the tourist frenzy.

João will provide attentive service and some lovely pestiscos.

☎ +351 284 326 855

3 PLACES TO SLEEP

HOTEL EVA
★ ★ ★ ★
Center

If you want to stay at Faro city center, Hotel Eva is an appealing option. Located by the marina with a panoramic view of the Ria Formosa nature reserve, this recently refurbished 4-star hotel provides a cozy stay. You shouldn't miss the rooftop swimming pool.

☎ +351 289 001 000
✉ rec.eva@ap-hotelsresorts.com

VILA VITA PARC RESORT & SPA
★ ★ ★ ★ ★
55KM

This amazing luxurious resort is placed right by the ocean. With a large landscaped area, it enables plenty of opportunities for sports, fitness, entertainment, and walks. There's a wide variety of accommodation and dining choices, with different themed rooms, suites, villas, and restaurants.

☎ +351 282 310 100
✉ reservas@vilavitaparc.com

CONRAD ALGARVE
★ ★ ★ ★ ★
15KM

Featuring an impressive infinity pool that blends with the Atlantic Ocean, this sumptuous hotel is set in the golfer's paradise Quinta do Lago.
With a contemporary design and exquisite decor, it boasts the sleekest spa in the south of Portugal. You'll also find 5 restaurants and bars.

☎ +351 289 350 700

BUCKET LIST

- ☐ Take a dip in the natural swimming pools in Alte (Loulé)
- ☐ Go on a boat trip to the Caves of Ponta da Piedade (D. Ana beach, Lagos)
- ☐ Taste a Morgadinho (pastry)
- ☐ Take the Faro Património Histórico pedestrian trail
- ☐ Go birdwatching at Ria Formosa Natural Park
- ☐ Swim to the impressive Benagil caves (Lagoa)
- ☐ Climb up to Ponta da Piedade lighthouse (Lagos)
- ☐ Leave your stone at Foia viewpoint (Monchique)
- ☐ Have a picnic at Caldas de Monchique
- ☐ Try a Mediterranean diet dish in Tavira
- ☐ Eat a Bola de Berlim at the beach (pastry)
- ☐ Take a walk at Deserta Island
- ☐ Taste Amêndoa Amarga (alcoholic drink)
- ☐ Watch the dolphins at Zoomarine
- ☐ Take a canoe tour along Ria Formosa (Faro)

SPECIAL DATES

- Ria Formosa Festival (late July, early August)
- FolkFaro – International Folclore Festival (August)
- Silves Medieval Fair (August)
- F Festival – Art and Culture Festival (August/September)
- City Day (September 7th – Municipal Holiday)
- Santa Iria Fair (late October)

SHOPPING

- Forum Algarve – National Road (EN) 103, 125km
- Rua de Santo António
- Rua Primeiro de Dezembro
- Rua Vasco da Gama

HOW TO GET TO

🚗 CAR
Porto: 🕐5h00 🛣A1, A10, A13, A2, A22
Lisboa: 🕐2h45 🛣A2, A22

🚆 TRAIN
Porto: 🕐5h30 🚆AP ➡ Faro
Lisboa: 🕐3h00 🚆AP ➡ Faro

🚌 BUS
Porto: 🕐8h00
Lisboa: 🕐3h15

ℹ CITY TRANSPORTATION
Bus: Próximo – www.proximo.pt

PRICE RATING

€ € € € €

127

THE 🧭
ISLANDS

AÇORES -
PONTA
DELGADA

North
Atlantic
Ocean

ADEIRA – FUNCHAL

FUNCHAL

Be hypnotized by this green and turquoise subtropical wonderland. Feel the energy flowing from the authentic ambiance of its miraculous and spectacular cliffs and ravines. Madeira's mild climate and its stunning, luxurious mountains will make you want to discover more. Its unspoiled beaches and the vibrancy of its flora give the Atlantic Pearl the reputation of paradise.

DID YOU KNOW THAT...

D. Sebastião, King of Portugal from 1568 on, mysteriously disappeared during the Alcácer-Quibir battle in Morocco (1578). History tells that D. Sebastião retreated to Arguim, an Atlantic island known for its volatility (appears and disappears from time to time). Before arriving at the island and submerging with it, the young king stuck his sword in the Cape of Garajau (Madeira) promising his return. It is told that the day D. Sebastião decides to reconquer his Kingdom, he will go for his sword and as soon as he gets it, Madeira will submerge in the deep ocean forever, as both islands cannot co-exist.

7 PLACES TO VISIT

1 PORTO MONIZ NATURAL POOLS
Natural swimming pools formed by volcanic lava and naturally filled with crystal-clear sea water.

2 ST. VICENTE CAVES AND VOLCANISM CENTER
One of the first caves of volcanic origin to be opened to the public in Portugal. It comprises an underground route of over 1km and offers a range of educational and entertaining displays.

3 CABO GIRÃO
The highest cape in Europe, at an elevation of 580m. Famous for its suspended glass platform – the skywalk.

4 STATUE OF CHRIST-KING AT GARAJAU (CANIÇO – SANTA CRUZ)
Statue of Christ with open arms facing the ocean. Located at the Ponta do Garajau viewpoint, offers an excellent partial view over Funchal bay.

5 MONTE PALACE BOTANICAL GARDEN
Located at the Quinta Monte Palace, this tropical garden is enriched with a 100,000 exotic plants collection.

6 PORTO SANTO BEACH (PORTO SANTO ISLAND)
A 9km beach with unique crystal-clear blue warm waters. One of the 7 Wonders – Beaches of Portugal.

7 CHAPEL OF NOSSA SENHORA DA GRAÇA (PORTO SANTO ISLAND)
One of the oldest churches in Porto Santo, dated before 1533.
Many of the island inhabitants used it as a place of refuge from pirates.

3 PLACES TO EAT

CRIS'S PLACE
Mediterranean

€ €

Don't be mistaken by the modest looking façade, Cris's Place provides a delightful dining experience. The quality of the food served, the premium service and the value of the concept menu will make you want to come back.

+351 291 762 263

WILLIAM RESTAURANT
Mediterranean

€ € €

Within Belmond Reid's Palace, boasting superb views of the coast, you'll find this Michelin-starred restaurant, which proposes a creative approach towards modern European food.

Chef Joachim Koerper will guarantee a feast not only for the mouth, but also for the eyes.

+351 291 717 171

IL GALLO D'ORO
Mediterranean

€ € €

Chef Benoît Sinthon creates well-heeled dinners with Mediterranean and Madeiran inspiration, sourcing most of the products from the local markets. Located inside the award-winning Cliff Bay Hotel, it continually proves itself for earning 2 Michelin stars.

+351 291 707 700

RESTAURANTE JAQUET
Tasca

You can't leave Madeira without trying their traditional seafood. Jaquet is a tiny restaurant by the fish market and has many rustic dishes available, peixe espada em vinha d' alhos (swordfish with vinegar and garlic) and lapas (limpets) being their main specialties.

+351 291 225 344

3 PLACES TO SLEEP

QUINTA JARDINS DO LAGO
★ ★ ★ ★ ★
Center

Erected in the 18th century, Quinta Jardins do Lago offers excellent hotel services with 31 rooms allied to an enormous historical and patrimonial wealth. Located near the center of Funchal, this hotel lays within a botanical garden (which holds more than 500 different species), providing an impressive view over the ocean.

+351 291 750 100

info@jardins-lago.pt

HOTEL PORTO MARE - PORTOBAY
★ ★ ★ ★
3KM

Occupying the center of the Porto Mare resort, this hotel boasts exuberant gardens that are enhanced by the island climate near the seaside promenade. It includes 5 pools and near 200 high-standard rooms. Regular buses to the city center are available.

+351 291 703 700

BELMOND REID'S PALACE
★ ★ ★ ★ ★
Center

This award-winning hotel is a breathtaking retreat overlooking the Atlantic Ocean. Existing for more than 125 years, it surprises with the luxury and charm of the common areas.

+351 291 71 71 71

BUCKET LIST

- [ ] Take one of the Levadas pedestrian trails
- [ ] Try Poncha da Madeira (alcoholic drink)
- [ ] Go on a boat trip to watch the dolphins, whales and monk seals
- [ ] Take a selfie with the bronze bust of Cristiano Ronaldo at Madeira's airport
- [ ] Take a walk at the Old Town and observe the Painted Doors Project
- [ ] Taste Bolo do Caco (traditional bread)
- [ ] Watch a Bailinho da Madeira performance/show
- [ ] Take a ride in one of the Island's cable cars
- [ ] Have a picnic at the Fanal leisure area (Laurissilva Forest Nature Reserve)
- [ ] Check out the view from Ponta do Rosto viewpoint
- [ ] Take a Monte sled ride (transport made of basketwork)
- [ ] Try fresh fruit from the Farmer's Market (Funchal)
- [ ] Go on a Blandy's Old Wine Lodges tour
- [ ] Taste a traditional honey cake (pastry)
- [ ] Take a picture in front of a typical Casa de Santana (Santana)

SPECIAL DATES

- Carnival Festivities (February)
- Flower Festival (April/May)
- Atlantic Festival (June)
- Madeira Wine Festival (late August, early September)
- Columbus Festival in Vila Baleira, Porto Santo Island (September)
- Nature Festival (October)
- New Year Festivities (December)

PRICE RATING

HOW TO GET TO

✈ PLANE
Porto: 🕐2h00
Lisboa: 🕐2h00

ℹ CITY TRANSPORTATION
Bus: Horários do Funchal – www.horariosdofunchal.pt/

SHOPPING

- Centro Comercial Anadia – Rua do Visconde de Anadia, 27
- Arcadas São Francisco Centro Comercial – Rua de São Francisco, 20
- Centro Comercial Galerias de São Lourenço – Avenida Arriaga, 45
- Centro Comercial La Vie – Rua Doutor Brito Câmara, 9
- Centro Comercial Madeira Shopping – Caminho Santa Quitéria, 44
- Rua Dr. Fernando de Ornelas
- Rua da Queimada de Cima

Create unforgettable memories anchored in the incomparable natural beauty of Açores. The fascinating volcanic presence and the dazzling lakes will provide you countless and exciting adventures. Submerge in the unhurried archipelago's pace of life and sense the antiquity of its colonial streets. Engage with the unmatched local traditions and be delighted by the rich gastronomy of the Islands.

DID YOU KNOW THAT...

During the Second World War, it was from the Lajes Air Base, in Terceira Island, that the Allies began to secure control of the North Atlantic and to ensure the safety of its freight transports. This fact allowed a strategic military relationship between the USA and Portugal that lasts until the present day.

Nowadays, in addition to its military function, the Lajes Air Base, is responsible for safeguarding the territorial waters of the Açores archipelago and works as a Coordinating Center for Search and Rescue.

7 PLACES TO VISIT

1 PONTA DELGADA HISTORICAL CENTER (SÃO MIGUEL ISLAND)

Houses and buildings whitewashed, churches and convents from the 17th and 18th centuries, cobbled narrow streets and small squares.

2 LAGOON OF SETE CIDADES (SÃO MIGUEL ISLAND)

Located in the volcanic craters that form the Island, the Lagoon of Sete Cidades is the most extensive freshwater lake in the entire Açores archipelago. It consists of two different lagoons – Green and Blue.

3 ST. JOÃO BAPTISTA FORTRESS (ANGRA DO HEROÍSMO – TERCEIRA ISLAND)

A fortress from the 17th century, built to protect the harbor of Angra do Heroísmo and shelter the colonial fleets from the pirates and corsairs' assaults.

4 VOLCANO CHIMNEY OF ALGAR DO CARVÃO (TERCEIRA ISLAND)

A vertical channel of about 45 meters that ends in a lagoon of clear water, at a depth of 80 meters. Embellished by exuberant and rare stalactites and stalagmites.

5 LANDSCAPE OF THE PICO ISLAND VINEYARD CULTURE

A network of long stone walls, spaced apart, running parallel to the coast and penetrating towards the interior of the Island. Erected to protect the vines from the wind and sea water.

6 GRUTA DAS TORRES IN PICO ISLAND

One of the most massive lava tubes in the world. It extends for 5km and presents various types of lava stalactites and stalagmites.

7 HEADLAND OF PONTA DOS CAPELINHOS (FAIAL ISLAND)

One of the few places where it is possible to observe what remains of the last manifestations of volcanic activity in Faial, back in 50's.

135

3 PLACES TO EAT

COLÉGIO 27 REST. & JAZZ CLUB
Mediterranean
€ €

Colégio 27 is a small bistro in the historical part of the city, created from a restored building that was once a stable.
The ambiance and live music fill a great experience, Jazz being the main attraction.

RESTAURANTE GASTRÓNOMO
Seafood
€ €

Considered one of the best restaurants in the Açores, Gastrónomo not only offers fresh fish, but it also excels in meat and shellfish dishes. Although the façade and the interior itself are unpretentious, the genuine local cuisine and hospitable staff largely compensate for that.
☎ +351 296 381 095

BEIRA MAR
Seafood
€ €

If you decide to travel to Angra do Heroísmo, Beira Mar has the freshest seafood there is. Placed right by the harbor, fishermen provide this establishment with superb ingredients for a genuine Azorean meal.
☎ +351 295 642 392

A TASCA
Tasca

This tasca is a mixture of regional cuisine and decor with some modern elements. Providing ambient music and live art, it's an exciting place to join a group of friends for some tidbits, including roasted tuna, limpets, sausages or octopus.
☎ +351 296 288 880

3 PLACES TO SLEEP

AZOR HOTEL
★ ★ ★ ★ ★
Center

Offering 123 rooms with fantastic views of the sea, Azor Hotel is a cosmopolitan establishment with an outdoor swimming pool located in Ponta Delgada, São Miguel Island.
Placed right at the harbor and about a 5-minute walk from the city center, this hotel is the best option for staying at the archipelago's main island.
☎ +351 296 249 900

TERRA NOSTRA GARDEN HOTEL
★ ★ ★ ★
Center

Located in a valley deep inside the São Miguel Island surrounded by trees, gardens and thermal springs, Terra Nostra offers a more relaxed and peaceful environment.
Recently decorated in Art Deco style, it merges elegantly with the natural surroundings.
Nearby you'll find volcanic beaches, a forest, and the Furnas Golf Course.

TERCEIRA MAR HOTEL
★ ★ ★ ★
Angra do Heroísmo

If you plan on staying in Terceira Island, this resort-style hotel will provide you the amenities you need and professional service. With a gorgeous ocean view, it is only a 15-minute walk from the historic city center, classified by UNESCO as World Heritage.
☎ +351 295 402 280

BUCKET LIST

- [ ] Take the Pico Alto pedestrian trail at Santa Maria Island
- [ ] Taste Caldo de Nabos from Santa Maria Island (soup)
- [ ] Go whale watching (São Miguel Island)
- [ ] Spend an afternoon at Terra Nostra Park in Furnas (São Miguel Island)
- [ ] Taste Cozidos das Furnas in São Miguel Island (meat or fish dish)
- [ ] Check out the view from Boca do Inferno viewpoint (São Miguel Island)
- [ ] Take a boat ride to visit the Islet of Vila Franca do Campo (São Miguel Island)
- [ ] Go horseback riding in São Miguel Island
- [ ] Taste the traditional pastry Queijadas de Vila Franca do Campo (São Miguel Island)
- [ ] Take the pedestrian trail of Fajã dos Vimes – Fragueira – Portal (São Jorge Island)
- [ ] Taste São Jorge Cheese (São Jorge Island)
- [ ] Swim in the lava pools of Biscoitos (Terceira Island)
- [ ] Go on a trip to Furna do Enxofre, sulfur cavern in Graciosa Island
- [ ] Go birdwatching at Flores Island
- [ ] Bathe in the thermal baths at Termas da Ferraria and in the pools in Furnas (São Miguel Island)

SPECIAL DATES

- Senhor Santo Cristo dos Milagres Festival in São Miguel Island (April/May)
- Velas Cultural Week in São Jorge Island (July)
- Sanjoaninas Festival in Terceira Island (late June)
- Senhor Bom Jesus Milagroso Festival in Pico Island (early August)
- Senhora dos Milagres Festival in Corvo Island (August 15th)
- Senhora da Guia Festival in Faial Island (August)
- Espírito Santo Festival, all islands (from April to September)

PRICE RATING

HOW TO GET TO

✈ PLANE
Porto: 🕐1h30
Lisboa: 🕐1h30

ℹ CITY TRANSPORTATION
Boat: Atlânticoline – www.atlanticoline.pt

SHOPPING

- Parque Atlântico – Rua da Juventude (Ponta Delgada, São Miguel Island)
- Rua Machado dos Santos (Ponta Delgada, São Miguel Island)
- Rua Direita (Angra do Heroísmo, Terceira Island)
- Rua da Sé (Angra do Heroísmo, Terceira Island)

PUBLISHED BY FOXHOUNDGLOBAL

1st edition – October 2018

ISBN 9780578402918